ARCHITECTURE AT THE EDGE OF EVERYTHING ELSE

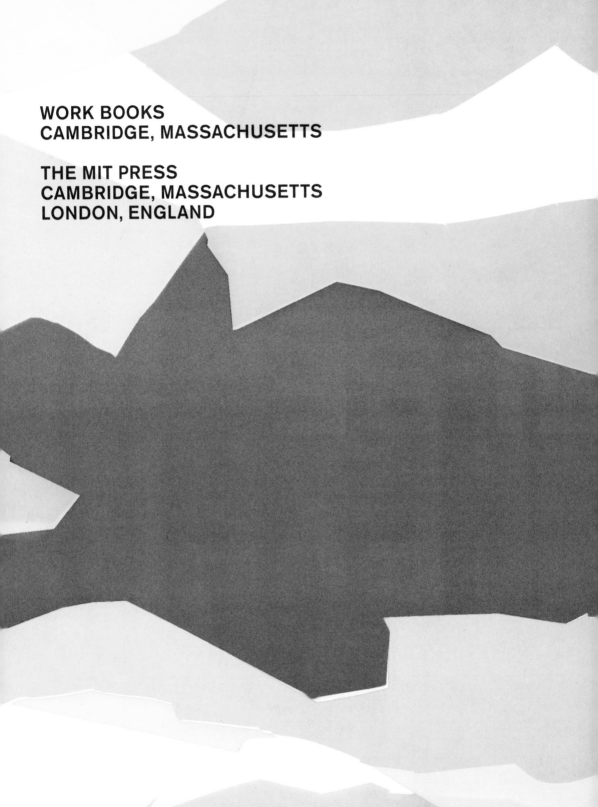

WORK BOOKS
CAMBRIDGE, MASSACHUSETTS

THE MIT PRESS
CAMBRIDGE, MASSACHUSETTS
LONDON, ENGLAND

ARCHITECTURE AT THE EDGE OF EVERYTHING ELSE

ESTHER CHOI &
MARRIKKA TROTTER,
EDITORS

MIT Press books may be purchased at special quantity discounts for business or sales promotional use. For information, please email special_sales@mitpress.mit.edu or write to Special Sales Department, The MIT Press, 55 Hayward Street, Cambridge, MA 02142.

The Work Books project was conceived by Esther Choi and Marrikka Trotter in 2008.

This book was printed and bound in China. Design: Omnivore, Inc.

Library of Congress Cataloging-in-Publication Data

Architecture at the edge of everything else / edited by Esther Choi and Marrikka Trotter.
     p. cm. — (Work books ; 1)
  Includes bibliographical references and index.
  ISBN 978-0-262-01479-3 (hardcover : alk. paper) 1. Architecture—Philosophy. I. Choi, Esther. II. Trotter, Marrikka.
  NA2500.A715 2010
  720.1—dc22
             2010011627

10   9   8   7   6   5   4   3   2   1

www.work-books.org

CONTENTS

Acknowledgements—

We would like to thank Roger Conover and his team at the MIT Press for believing in this publication and for spurring us to do better, go farther and never settle. The contributors to this book signed on when there was no real likelihood that the project would come to fruition, and they stuck with this process with generosity, tenacity and understanding throughout. In particular, we owe a special debt of gratitude to Sanford Kwinter, who was a stalwart supporter and unofficial advisor for this project from the beginning. We would like to thank Breanne Woods, our design collaborator on the vision document; Judith McKay, our project manager; and especially our designers, Omnivore. Their expertise and guidance during the design process was essential. We are also grateful to Wim Delvoye, Foster + Partners, Gensler, Dan Hui, Nike Media Relations, Paula Cooper Gallery, Julia Rothman, Guy Wenborne and Yonezawa City Uesugi Museum for their generous help with images. Our sincere appreciation goes to our Flickr photographers, Bruno Bellec, David Brittain, Melody Kramer, Manuela Martin and Aimin Wang. To Ben Playford and Jonathan Santos, our thanks for your unconditional patience, love and support.

THE NAME OF THE GAME

A conversation between Esther Choi and Marrikka Trotter, editors

Esther Choi— Coming from a non-architectural background,
I have always admired the way that many architectural
practitioners took the initiative to create their own
platforms for discussion. The proliferation of 'little magazines' in the 1960s and 1970s was particularly
inspiring because these publications echoed the DIY
aesthetics and fanzine production approach that were so
central to subcultural communication and activism within
adjacent disciplines. Of course, the same activity was
going on in the disciplines of art criticism and production at the time, but the architectural tendency to treat
theory and practice as coextensive threads of the same
creative enterprise outlasted similar efforts in other
fields. Few contemporary artists wear the critic/theorist
hat, but it is still common for architects to contribute
to both design and discourse. So when we met as students
at Harvard's Graduate School of Design, I was disap-
pointed to see that the majority of young practitioners
and architecture students were hesitant to claim that
tradition for themselves or to redefine it in a way that
would be of relevance to them.

Marrikka Trotter— I attended a roundtable discussion at
the GSD when Peter Sloterdijk made a comment that caused
a lot of students to actually tear up. He pointed out
that while his (post-WWII) generation had been impressed
upon that they mattered and that they had an important
role to play in the world, young people today are being
made to feel that they have neither the capacity within
themselves nor the historical-cultural-political room in
the world to make a contribution. He was very sad about
that, and he was in some ways accusing his own generation. He said something to the effect of "we have to tell
students today that they are vital—that we *need* them
and their ideas." I'm not willing to cast blame on baby
boomers en masse, but our predecessors were born into an
era of epic struggle. And in 1968 or thereabouts, when a
lot of liberal thinkers felt like they lost their fight
to change the fundamental operations of the world, it's
not only as if they hammered their own swords into plowshares, but also the only thing they taught us to do was
to make more plowshares while attending carefully to
stories about the glory days. There's a limit to how many
agricultural implements and good note-takers are useful at any one time in history. In reality, there are so
many extraordinarily urgent and necessary issues that new
minds and new approaches need to try to address.

EC— And yet there's a deep hesitation on the part of architecture to engage with adjacent forms of cultural production, despite the fact that these fields are embedded and historically intertwined within the discipline. It's common for architectural historians and critics to diminish contributions from well-respected art historians and critics to architectural discourse, as if these outside perspectives could only offer "less." Architectural thinkers sometimes seem committed to an infantilizing attitude toward other disciplines, which is a strange pretense considering that architecture as a practice is inherently collaborative, polyphonic, and dispersed. Curator Kelly Baum has suggested that heterogeneity can provide a structural logic as well as act as the subject for contemporary art practices—and I'd like to think about this book as an experiment at putting that divergent, inclusive, and "agonistic" theory into practice within the architectural discipline.[1]

1— See Kelly Baum, "Questionnaire on 'The Contemporary,'" *October* 130 (Fall 2009): 94.

MT— Exactly. Look at how the discipline of architecture as a body has reflected both the influences it likes to think it chooses—ideas and images from philosophy, art, and science (in a one-way direction, of course, as you point out)—and the contamination it cannot avoid, like legislative constraints and the flow of finance. The former is habitually applied to the surface of architectural production as "clothing" of discursive terminology and formal or aesthetic effects. The latter infects and modifies like germs or gravity, changing not the terms used within the discourse but, rather, forms of thinking—affecting not the fashion of architecture but its modes of practice. We are inundated with examples of the first kind of influence; these are trumpeted. An example of the second kind of contamination might be specifications, which have exponentially expanded in length and complexity in the past one hundred years until they have reached the limit state of unwieldiness at the same time that their production consumes an inordinate amount of energy. The liability involved in the production of built work has pooled within the corpus of architecture simply because it could not be fought off. I would like to see the exchange and interchange between architecture and its surrounding vectors become two-way in each kind of contamination and influence, so that architecture is confined neither to superficiality nor to subservience. There's a misplaced sense of translation in which an argument and its revelatory potential are deployed by the discipline into an alibi for a form-making methodology. Architecture is not (inherently) a crime: it does not (inherently) need an alibi.

One thing that I think is becoming clearer, even though it's usually unstated, is that there is a new willingness to separate the profession from the activity and discourse of architecture. I think this book is beginning to map this fissure. People are willing to explore deploying architectural ideas or architectural techniques outside the profession.

EC— But isn't that problematic in terms of the social relevance of architecture?

MT— I don't think so, because I think the profession of architecture is losing its value in the world of today. I'm making a distinction between the architectural discipline and the architectural profession. I don't think that the discipline is going away, just that the profession has less and less to offer. The profession started out as an essential mechanism for a certain mode of economic and political operation that has lost its value and has almost ceased to exist. This doesn't mean that we're in any danger of losing the specificity of architectural procedures, but merely that we are getting to the point where we can no longer sustain the separation of architecture *as a profession* from all other creative activity. I like Michael Meredith and Liam Gillick's definition of the discipline and discourse of architecture versus art. In their conversation they conclude that anything can be defined as architectural so long as architects are talking about it, and that the same holds true for art. That makes a lot of sense to me; it depends on to whom you are talking and who is listening.

EC— But surely that is still a move to continue to treat architecture as autonomous within a much larger field of spatial practices. I would rather frame architecture as an extension of these other practices because it creates a more heterogeneously inclusive model that could include what Michael and Liam pointedly disavowed: an eclectic array of practices and diverse modes of investigation in general. There's no question that collaborations and conversations across disciplines can result in potentially fruitful advances. With the steady divergence between architecture's practice and profession that you spoke of, architects are increasingly infiltrating spaces like galleries and museums more typical to artistic practices as they seek sites for architectural experimentation. I'm not advocating that we

dissolve disciplinary boundaries simply because of novel
formal or institutional similarities that may exist
between architecture and other forms of cultural production, but I don't think that these congruencies can be
disregarded either. There are a number of historically
rich moments of overlap between art and architecture—
from Lilly Reich and Mies van der Rohe's 1927 Velvet and
Silk Café to Gordon Matta Clark's building cuts of the
1970s—and these episodes of methodological and disciplinary cross-pollination demonstrate how the blurring
of boundaries can cause a third condition from which new
questions and imaginative modes of practice and thought
may emerge. Regardless of whether we agree or disagree
with the notion of broadening disciplinary frameworks
to consider a larger field of spatial practices, there
are a growing number of contemporary architectural and
artistic practices that seek to intentionally exacerbate
the intermittent and ambiguous connections between art,
architecture, commerce, politics, and the social realm.
Both theorists and practitioners need to develop new
vocabularies for understanding and interpreting these
modes of practice; in turn, new audiences will emerge.
For me, the question is not how or why we should delin-
eate disciplinary boundaries, but rather, how we can
perforate disciplinary boundaries without eroding the
discipline and rigor with which our intellectual inves-
tigations should be undertaken.

MT— There is a difference in understanding how things
contaminate and infect each other and believing that
contamination or infectiousness somehow has the power
to erode the individuality of the body that is concerned. Just because I have a million different organisms infecting my body does not mean that I do not have
an identity. It might mean that they kill me, but that's
another discussion.

I know how to detail a window and you don't. You know
how to design a light installation and I don't. But I'm
not going to suddenly forget how to detail a window
because I'm talking to you. All that I risk is education. "Interdisciplinary" in this context just means that
disciplines are talking among themselves. It doesn't mean
nondisciplinary. If it's nondisciplinary, then I agree
that we have a problem. But if you have an architect who
is doing art, then either that architect is talking to
architects through the medium of art or the architect is
also an artist and therefore also participating in art
discourse. But the mediums still exist—it's always going

to be either one or the other, even when some people do both. So, for me, people are afraid of the wrong thing.

EC— Absolutely. In terms of the pragmatic implementation of interdisciplinary thinking and action within the architectural discipline, there seem to be two major factors: on the one hand, there is reluctance on the part of institutions and architectural practitioners to release themselves from their self-imposed disciplinary autonomy and challenge their attitudes toward ideas and forces from outside the discipline. On the other hand, impacting any kind of change at this level involves allowing other voices to enter the conversation. It's striking that the few prominent figures who were not trained as architects, namely Sanford Kwinter and Jeffrey Kipnis, have made such provocative contributions to architectural discourse, yet the paucity of platforms for cross- or trans- or inter-disciplinary conversations persists.

MT— That lack of platforms points to a lack of initiative, and the lack of initiative brings us right back to where we started this conversation. That's part of the project of Work Books: we are trying to elucidate and work through ideas, not because we want to develop ideological positions free from contamination, but rather because we want to understand and participate in what is underway. I'd like to think about our platform as a desk—not something that you stand on but a surface for work—containing different tools and different projects in various states of completion. I want people to feel free to bring their work to the desk and work on it with other people.

EC— One of the larger strains emerging from the book, not in a polemical sense, but in terms of a shared concern, deals with the issue of *agency*. This word comes up repeatedly throughout the book, and I think it speaks to a much larger concern among younger practitioners about the role that architecture plays in instigating interventions within the public realm and imagining particular forms of social possibility. Various political theories dealing with participation and relational practices are referenced as a way to think about the nature of social relationships and the kinds of environments that engender these relationships. I've found that this topic of agency is delivered with a sense of "authenticity" and insistence. I keep returning to Andrew Zago's idea of "post-ironic authenticity"[2]—and I'd like to think of this book as

2— See Andrew Zago, "Real What?" *Log* 5 (Spring/Summer 2005): 101.

a response to that call. The contributors in this volume seem to be loosely affiliated around an interest in
resisting *inertia*.

MT— I agree. We need a myriad of people, approaches,
tactics, and ideas, all deploying in whatever space and
whatever capacity possible. This is not a monolithic
ideological effort but rather an incremental, ongoing,
and very diffuse project of trying to realize something
better than what we see in front of us. You can take that
politically, economically, or ecologically.

It's funny because we talked about all of the threads
that connect the essays in a positive manner, but one
thing that also connects them in a negative sense is a
complete rejection of the so-called postcritical project.
I think it *should* be rejected and hope it's gone away.
But even though we have contributor after contributor
identifying reasons that postcriticality is insufficient
or problematic, in the end I think we produced a
projective book. People are actually projecting new
possibilities into the larger discourse. In terms of
platforms, this book is our performative *book* act: the
doing of it makes it so.

HOW TO INTERPRET

Esther Choi

How Does It Feel to Feel?

The scarcity of agitation is agitating.
—Jeffrey Inaba[1]

In harmony with the sixties' chemically induced interaction with the world, a British psychedelic freakbeat band called The Creation released a single that posed the question: "*how does it feel to feel?*"[2] While other musical groups extolled the mood evoked by indulgence in stimulants—veiling languor with hallucinatory theatre—The Creation's raucous litany described the unsavory experience of narcotic withdrawal. Their tribute was less an anthem lauding the ecstatic pleasures of sedative special effects than a repetitious refrain that underscored the conflictive aspects of sensation. They asked:

How does it feel when you wake in the morning?
How does it feel feeling sun in the shade?
How does it feel when you slide down a sunbeam?
How does it feel bursting clouds on your way?
How does it feel now that the night is over?
How does it feel never to sleep again?
How does it feel to feel?[3]

1— Jeffrey Inaba, "Agitation," *Volume* 10 (2006): 2.

2—For the purposes of my argument, I will refer specifically to the first iteration of The Creation (1966–1968) and not the diluted variations of the band after this period, along with their most representative songs, "Painter Man," "Making Time" and "How Does It Feel to Feel."

3—The Creation, *How Does It Feel To Feel*, The Creation. Performed 1967. Original sound recording made by Hit-ton Schallplatten (Germany), Vinyl HT 300 102 (7") and rereleased in 1968 by Polydor (UK). Vinyl 56230.

The song's systematic word play referenced the slippage between the oppositional states of pleasurable and agonistic experience, obscuring and unsettling the relationship between the two. This nexus between delight and discontent was a central facet of The Creation's auditory approach. Unlike more reactionary musical genres like punk, psychedelic freakbeat incorporated contrasting yet gradated inflections of memorable, harmonious melodies together with moments of cacophonous guitar feedback and exaggerated fuzz tone. Devoid of insipid posturing, The Creation's attitude towards aural abrasion also embodied a form of "pre-ironic authenticity" that promoted an earnest, unassuming restraint rather than self-effacing or entropic narratives.[4] In contrast to other British counterculture acts of the time, many of their songs were clumsy, pounding declarations performed with unapologetic insistence.

Although acclaimed guitarists like Jimi Hendrix demonstrated "virtuoso technique"[5] and performers like David Bowie employed the cosmetic as an "instrumental tactic,"[6] The Creation's unrefined musicality engaged in an alchemic approach to administering delightful effects of visceral damage.[7]

Like the LSD-inspired love ballads of the sixties, the affective turn in architectural discourse has been used in equally reductive ways to denote the convivial, gratifying and hedonic registers of sensation.[8] Increasingly, contemporary discussions concerning projective strategies of architectural practice have signaled an interest in wielding superficial material effects to induce these presumably pleasurable forms of feeling. Resembling slacker aesthetics in contemporary art, the projective proposal has embraced the use of environment-altering moods, performances and ambiences in an effort to elevate unimaginative complicity to the level of subterfuge,

4— I use the phrase "pre-ironic authenticity" to make reference to Andrew Zago's essay, "Real What?" published in *Log* 5 (Spring/ Summer 2005): 101–105.

5—Sanford Kwinter and Jeffrey Kipnis have suggested that the techniques of Hendrix's guitar playing can be used as a methodological armature for architectural practice.

6—Jason Payne, "Hair and Make Up," *Log* 17 (2004): 41.

7—While lead guitarist Eddie Phillips's contribution to guitar playing has been largely disregarded and overshadowed by figures like Pete Townsend, his experiments with feedback and noise with The Creation resulted in the enormous influence The Creation had on the development of garage and punk rock music in Britain and the United States.

8—While in psychological terms "hedonics" implies the gamut of affects ranging from pleasantness to unpleasantness, many artists and architects have interpreted it to be strictly concerned with aspects of the pleasure principle. My use of the term in this essay is in reference to this one-dimensional interpretation of the concept. See Barbara Maria Stafford, "Hedonics," in *Sensorium: Embodied Experience, Technology, and Contemporary Art*, ed. Caroline A. Jones (Cambridge: MIT Press, 2006), 149–153. In her brief article, Stafford puts forth the suggestion that hedonics, the range of pleasurable and displeasing states used in psychology, has been a central component to the discourse of art since the Enlightenment. A recent interest in hedonics has been initiated by hedonic contingency theory, which correlates cognitive flexibility and creative

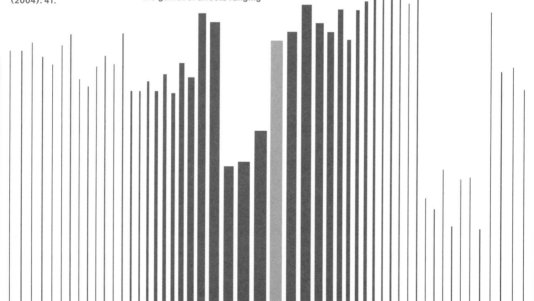

bracketing potential concerns without any allegiance to larger commitments.[9] Framing the production and the consumption of these effects as "cool" and easy enterprises, this approach is rooted in the cosmetic dimensions of material reality.[10]

ability in relation to various registers of positive mood. See also Edward R. Hirt, Erin E. Devers, and Sean M. McCrea, "I Want to Be Creative: Exploring the Role of Hedonic Contingency Theory in the Positive Mood–Cognitive Flexibility Link," *Journal of Personality and Social Psychology* 94, no. 2 (2008): 214–230.

9—Johanna Drucker's summation of artist Jason Rhoades's installation art and its slackeresque sensibility can easily act as a précis of the projective practice proposed by Robert Somol and Sarah Whiting: "This

work has no more to it than meets the eye. No redeeming arguments will transform these installations into works of profound aesthetic value in formal or critical terms. Quite the contrary, these two installations are ephemeral and transitory." See Johanna Drucker, *Sweet Dreams: Contemporary Art and Complicity* (Chicago: University of Chicago Press, 2005), 95.

10—Robert Somol and Sarah Whiting, "Notes Around the Doppler Effect and Other Moods of Modernism," *Perspecta* 33 (2002): 73–74.

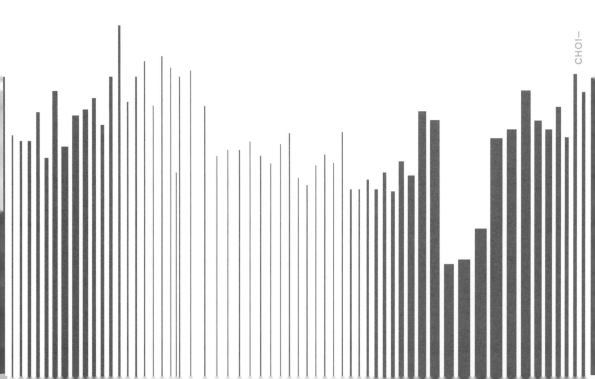

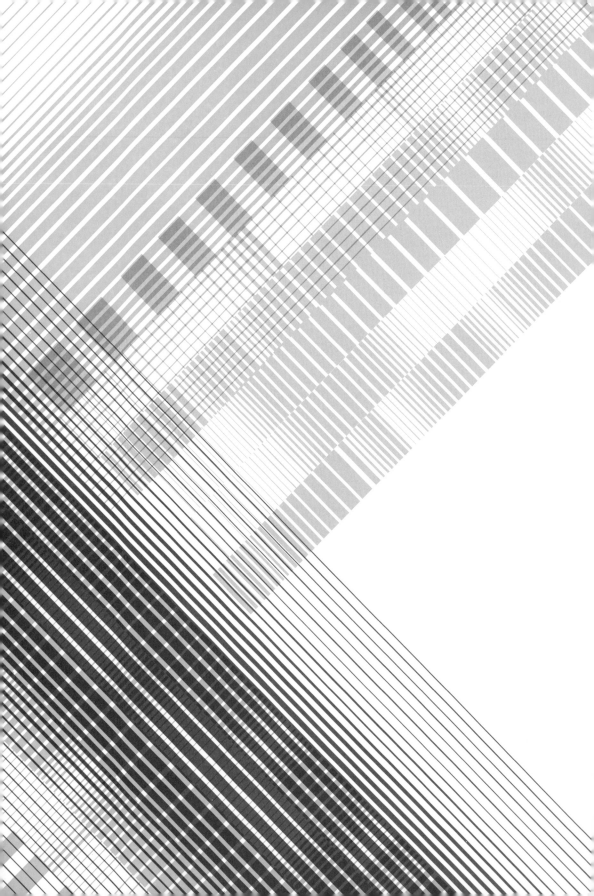

Architecture could learn from psyche-delic freakbeat. Vitruvius wrote that build-ing must possess the qualities of firmness, commodity and *delight*, but his emphasis on architecture's responsibility to produce pleasure risks losing sight of the limitations posed by immediate aesthetic gratification; temporary illusions are incapable of sustaining any deeper meaning. Unlike other disciplines intrinsically connected to the affective realm—such as music and art—the architectural disci-pline has yet to acknowledge the full gamut of sensation ranging from delight to disturbance. In lieu of triggering a singular affective register within the nebulous constellation of feeling, freakbeat used conflictive dynamics—found in The Creation's musical combination of pleas-ing melodies and discordant effects—as a way of understanding the ambient topographies of sensation. Freakbeat's alchemic orchestra-tion of divergent elements served to enhance, texturize and invent new tones and rhythms. As a genre, it employed the tempered admission of sensation's negative registers to expose new possibilities for unsettling complexity; in turn, this complexity reflected the intricate and contrasting emotional registers that are central to human experience.

From a biological standpoint, the act of feeling is a physical system's process of "grappling" with variance in order to resist the inertia of its ongoing mechanics.[11] During the process of experiencing affect, a body's sys-tem is disrupted by a change or transformation that literally *affects* it, and in turn, these affects exert force or pressure which may engender reactions on both cognitive and behavioral levels, enabling new forms of performance, states and habits to be produced.[12] Conflictive dynamics are the basis for the generation of all affective responses; biological organisms, including sentient human beings, are con-tinually engaged in contestatory struggles to maintain the cohesion of their selfhood and territory. Although encountering friction may

momentarily constrain the body and the brain, these frustrations are a necessary condi-tion for engendering new forms of resistance within all biological systems. This takes place through ever-fluctuating homeostatic activ-ity involving varying intensities of functional stress that occur within an organism's struc-ture and ultimately determine the distribution of resources and energy on the part of the organism—including its behavior, cognition and bodily reflexes.[13] Affects are thus rooted in an organism's drive for survival.[14] As "becomings," they possess the capacity to produce potential emergent effects, ultimately determining how a body may *feel* and thus how a body may *act* and what a body may *do*.

Friction is a crucial force for our under-standing of the world and our ability to form co-extensive engagements within it. In order to understand subjectivity and feeling as "pat-terns in space and time," it is useful to frame affective responses as forms of system disrup-tion.[15] David Rudrauf and Antonio Damasio have argued that an "affective system" is organized using an "agonistic logic" where disequilibrium is the basis for an organism's resistance of inertia.[16] Disequilibrium is caused by a distribution of deviances or alterations

11—David Rudrauf and Antonio Damasio, "A Conjecture Regarding the Biological Mechanism of Subjectivity and Feeling," *Journal of Consciousness Studies* 12, no. 8–10 (2005): 236.

12—"Affects generally exert a force of pres-sure on cognition and behaviour, modify them and require adaptation in order to endeavour in current routines and tasks, shift to other states, or simply face them. This pressure or tension itself is a central component of what we feel." Rudrauf and Damasio, "A Conjecture," 242. They are referencing Robert E. Thayer's works,

The Biopsychology of Mood and Activation (New York: Oxford University Press, 1989), and *The Origins of Everyday Moods: Managing Energy, Tension, and Stress* (New York: Oxford University Press, 1996), as well as Aaron Ben-Ze'ev, *The Subtlety of Emotions* (Cambridge: MIT Press, 2000).

13—Ibid., 242–243.

14—Antonio Damasio, *Looking for Spinoza: Joy, Sorrow, and the Feeling Brain* (Orlando: Harcourt Inc., 2003), 40.

15—Rudrauf and Damasio, "A Conjecture," 238.

16—Ibid., 242.

operating as a range of intensities throughout the body's somatosensory faculties. Rudrauf and Damasio describe this arrangement as "a system with a general dynamical organization in which something resists, attempts to control its own transformations in an eventually very complex patterned way [creating a] … dynamical regime of resistance to variance."[17] As a principle of organization, disequilibrium offers a spatial model for architecture that is not formal but alchemic in nature, involving proportional combinations of effects to produce fluctuating dynamic states and complex interactions which are both spontaneous and transformative. The resulting technique could be akin to producing a "chemical space"[18] that operates on both biophysical and phenomenological levels, rooted not in the didacticism of material arrangements but in the application of an affective logic to architectonic expression.

While the vomit reflex supposedly provoked by Peter Eisenman's buildings offers one extreme example of how architecture may seek to generate affects within a continuum of intensities, I am instead advocating an architecture that practices a modulated and tempered approach to the affective realm, in which subtle gradients of contrasting sensation can commingle in a purposeful way. Like guitar-effects pedals, these layers of sensory distortions can be remixed to produce an ever-changing composition of variables and perturbations. The use of disequilibrium as an organizational principle advances a micro-political understanding of affect by enabling new formations of the affective and the political to take place. In other words, conflictive dynamics can allow architecture to stake its claim in the territories of the political project and the projective project alike.

As a literal depiction of this concept, Architecture Principe's Church Sainte-Bernadette du Banlay (1966) in Nevers, France, is a built manifesto of what collaborators Claude Parent and Paul Virilio termed "the function of the oblique." Parent and Virilio argued that the deployment of inclined planes within architecture created an important instability through the displacement of weight and mass; the fluctuating changes caused by both the acceleration and deceleration in one's body to adapt to these shifting slopes would result in an individual in a constant state of resistance.[19]

Borrowing an iconic vocabulary inspired by German bunkers, the mass of the church appears to float on the surface of the earth like a building without a foundation while inside, gravity and mass amplify each other to provoke a persistent and escalating feeling of opposition within an individual.[20] The fractured hexagonality of the plan merges two shells that obliquely overlap; the altar and sanctuary are situated on the double inverse slope of the ground plane, while the confessionals, instructional spaces, meeting rooms and parochial chamber are located one level below. The resulting effect is a felt experience of physical uncertainty that shifts the focus away from architecture as an object and toward the nature of the journey it initiates in space.[21] Creating an analogy between military and

17—Ibid., 244.

18—In reference to the work of Petra Blaisse, Sanford Kwinter has proposed that "chemical space" is "concerned with processes, probabilities, interactions and transformation." Sanford Kwinter, "The Garden and the Veil," Inside/Outside: Petra Blaisse, ed. Kayoko Ota (Rotterdam: NAi Publishers, 2006), 500.

19—Enrique Limon, "Paul Virilio and the Oblique," in Virilio Live: Selected Interviews, ed. John Armitage (London: Sage Publications Ltd., 2001), 53.

20—Paul Virilio, "Bunker Archaeology," in Function of the Oblique: The Architecture of Claude Parent and Paul Virilio 1963–1969, ed. Pamela Johnston

(London: The Architectural Association, 1996), 71.

21—Paul Virilio, "Architecture Principe," in Function of the Oblique, 13. The German art historian August Schmarsow also theorized that aesthetic experience is forged through a subject's embodied or empathetic response (Einfühlung) to produce an "aesthetic from within." See August Schmarsow, "The Essence of Architectural Creation" (1893), in Empathy, Form and Space: Problems in German Aesthetics, eds. Robert Vischer, et al., trans. Harry Francis Mallgrave, Eleftherios Ikonomou (Santa Monica: Getty Center for the History of Art and the Humanities, 1994), 281–297.

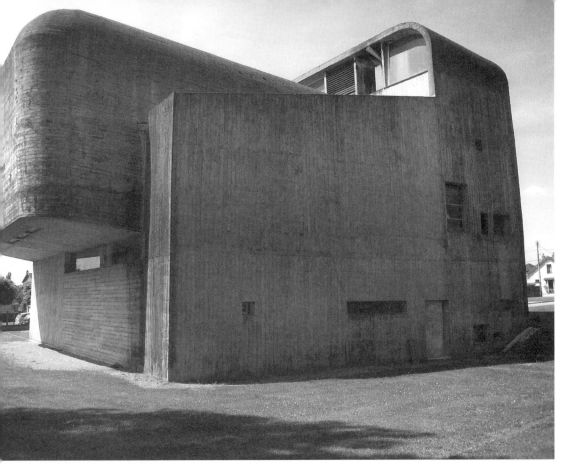

Architecture Principe, Church Sainte-
Bernadette du Banlay, Nevers,
France, 1966.

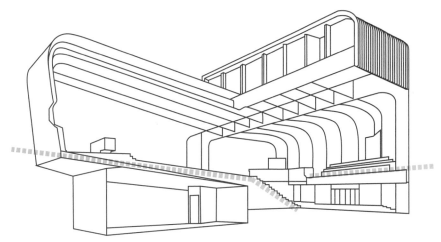

spiritual warfare, architecture becomes a blitz-krieg operation where a series of maneuvers works as part of a larger geopolitical strategy: an exercise in political-spatial geometry.[22]

The conceptual artist Hans Haacke also explored the political possibility of agonistic effects in his exhibition *Weather, Or Not*, which took place on the fourth floor of X, a temporary nonprofit art initiative that repurposed the Dia Art Foundation's former location in Chelsea.[23] Responding to X's site, a raw, uninhabited warehouse building, Haacke played with the space's haunting vacancy by creating a subtly uncomfortable environment. Opening all of the windows in the space and installing a wall of whirling industrial fans, Haacke allowed the winter breeze to permeate the gallery, creat-ing a somaesthetic experience for the pre-sentation of his work. Employing a loose and spacious configuration of artworks, *Weather, Or Not* was rife with a sense of abandonment. In light of the recent global economic crisis, the pairing of previously and recently pro-duced works dealing with corporate corruption and phantasmagoric depictions of moments of devastating financial mismanagement throughout history operated like the ghostly echoes of a feedback loop. While many of the appropriated images and texts made refer-ence to surplus power and wealth, Haacke exacerbated their meaning by demonstrating that the discordant reverberations of material wealth and power are *largely felt but not seen*. By employing climatic effects to connect the literal site of the gallery to its larger socio-economic and discursive contexts—thereby causing the autonomy of the gallery space to wane—Haacke supplanted didactic condemna-tion and declaration with conflictive sensory forces or "distortions" that operated on an ambient level beyond linguistic or textual nar-ratives. The show implicated the viewer in a

critical remapping of the matrices of power, autonomy and wealth by presenting a scenario whereby authority and agency were distributed to the audience in more open-ended ways. *Weather, Or Not*'s agonistic weather functioned as a mechanism for translating the effects of dissentient immaterial relations into a visceral atmosphere of administered affects and *sen-sory damage*.

In an essay published in 1984, Hal Foster circuitously investigated the concept of the political in order to "reconceive the project of [the then-contemporary] political art."[24] In his discussion of productivist models, Foster cites Walter Benjamin's rallying cry in "Author as Producer" for the artist to critically assess his/her alignment with the production process—that is, as Foster writes, "more than speak *for* this new social force, he must align his practice *with* its production."[25] Foster argues that previous incarnations of the productivist agenda (Russian productivism, the Bauhaus, and so forth) succeeded in reassigning the ratios of power and divisions of cultural labor to instantiate a type of entropic narrative of cultural production: this program was able to "turn workers into producers of art and free the artist and intellectual from the 'impossible place' of 'benefactor and ideological patron,'" to reestablish familiar and reflexive methods, and to encourage "a new model of meaning as actively produced, not … passively (i.e., institu-tionally) received."[26]

22—Limon, "Paul Virilio and the Oblique," 53.

23—Hans Haacke, *Weather, Or Not*, exhibition at X-Initiative, New York, November 21, 2009 through January 30, 2010.

24—Hal Foster, "For a Concept of the Political in Contemporary Art," in *Recodings: Art, Spectacle, Cultural Politics* (Seattle: Bay Press,1985), 144.

25—Ibid. 141.

26—Walter Benjamin, "The Author as Producer." in *The Essential Frankfurt School Reader*, eds. Andrew Arato and Eike Gebhardt (New York: Urizen Books, 1978), 268; quoted in Ibid., 141–142.

Hans Haacke, *The Invisible Hand of the Market*, 2009.

Hans Haacke, *Recording of Climate in Art Exhibition*, 1969-1970/ 2009.

Hans Haacke, *BONUS-Storm*, 2009.

Similarly, by broadening notions of how affective responses can be wielded to engender challenging experiments that operate in an oppositional or demanding manner, both Architecture Principe's "oblique manifesto" and Haacke's exhibition reconceived the value of agonistic modes of sensory disruption. In both scenarios, the deployment of affective transference served to question the assumed relationship between producer and audience by summoning participants to imagine individual and collective bodies as literal and functional sites for critiquing the efficacy of political power and practice.[27] Politics, in this case, is less a Marxist critique of class or a postmodern analysis of social representation than a nascent exploration of the way in which the political can be understood as the physiological, affective engagement of a body, instantiated through the aesthetic realm and in relation to its encounter with and generation of various potentials. Following Foster's analysis, my proposal does not advocate a reductive return to a productivist model, in which all "becomings" are seen to be *inherently productive*, but rather seeks to account for the consumption of and interaction with environmental stimuli and how these, too, may be culturally coded and informed by registers of difference.

Haacke's installation in particular can be interpreted as but one application of conflict as a spatial model, in which disequilibrium can paradoxically act as a form of connective tissue between the micro and macro. What is striking in this example is the way this strategy connects multiple isomorphic frameworks, spheres, and scales ranging from the biophysical, the neural, the subjective, the architectural, the aesthetic, the political, and the climatory, to the economic and the emotional. The resulting effect is a dynamic organizational model for how complex systems can be embodied and embedded within other circuitous frameworks, producing a spatial system in which the description of these isomorphic

27—I borrow the term "functional site" from James Meyer. For a more elaborate discussion of literal versus functional sites, see James Meyer, "The Functional Site; or, The Transformation of Site Specificity," in *Space, Site, Intervention: Situating Installation Art*, ed. Erika Suderberg (Minneapolis: University of Minnesota Press, 2000), 23–37.

28—Rudrauf and Damasio, "A Conjecture," 239. Rudrauf and Damasio write, "The problem is to understand and model one 'complex' level of the phenomenology–the subjective phenomenology—in the framework of another 'complex' phenomenological level—the description of an embodied being undergoing multiscale biophysical transformations."

29—Ibid., 244. "Just as it is certainly the case that a living organism is shaped and kept alive as a result of such ongoing action and reactions, it is conceivable that a subject or self is shaped and maintained only as a result of ongoing actions and reactions. Without the dynamics that lead to conflict between a level of control and a level of perturbation, the body could not be animated. And there is evidence suggesting that without proper operation and control of such basic dynamics the individual organism cannot survive autonomously and the self and consciousness dissolve. Coma, vegetative states, and akinetic mutism are extreme illustrations of the consequences on subjectivity and consciousness of the breakdown in the integral conflictive dynamics of action and reaction which makes a wakeful, vigilant, attentive and emoting individual. Maintaining life implies a struggle and cognition is yet another set of mechanisms for that struggle."

networks mirrors the manifold registers of sensation.[28] Disequilibrium is an approach that is not hostile to human subjectivity (à la Eisenman's aspirational vomit reflex); instead, it offers one possibility for how architecture can be deployed in symbiosis with biological systems, operating within logics of ongoing incongruity and agonism that incorporate the dynamics of human beings and the manner in which they experience. To return to the connection between conflictive dynamics and survival, it is feasible to conceive that a subject or living organism is formed and sustained *as a result of* continuous affects and reactions— without the agonistic forces that initiate varying levels of discord, the integrity of the body and its potential are subsumed.[29]

The resurgence of the affective turn in architecture affords practitioners the opportunity to reimagine how the discipline's use of material effects can be manipulated to erode the nonexistent and 'easy' relations between effects and their meaning. Similarly, projective architectural practice and theory must resist the effortlessly consumable modes of the convivial, the cool, the acquiescent and the "merely decorative,"[30] in order to reflect the relevant situational framework that architecture presently inhabits. What I wish to propose is a model of *architecture as a living system*: one that is shaped by the logic of an "affective interface" which is constantly active, continuously built and rebuilt, and which behaves in a responsive manner to novel differences.[31] This is but one methodology for exploring how architecture may innovatively relocate meaning: the theatrical nature of its material effects can be exercised to provoke a wider gamut of sensory interplays in aberrant, experimental and demanding ways, while simultaneously performing on multiple scales of sensation and action.

30—George Baird, "Criticality and Its Discontents," *Harvard Design Magazine* 21 (Fall 2004/Winter 2005): 6.

31—Rudrauf and Damasio, "A Conjecture," 243.

CHOI—

Neither Sweet nor Sour—

A conversation between Sylvia Lavin and Brett Albert

Brett Albert— On March 5, 2008, Dave Hickey gave a lecture at Harvard called "Graft Design: Collaborating with Clients and Codes," in which he characterized the GSD as a stronghold of labored resistance to the realities of architectural production, where students are still "hung up on Mies" and reference Benjamin and Derrida in their pin-ups. By way of contrast, he celebrated the model of LA-based firm Graft, which he said only needs and only has "one idea" (which boiled down to the realization of derivative surface geometries with rib structures). According to Hickey, this office effectively achieves that idea because of a willingness to embrace and exploit the limits of professional practice.

Though given by an art critic with what appeared to be a distorted image of our discipline, the lecture exemplified the way I think the paradigm of postcriticality has been abused in contemporary discourse. I don't believe that architecture schools today are the bastions of theoretical vanguardism that they are made out to be, even on the East Coast. Personally I have found a pervasive *disinterest* in theory in relation to work being produced in design studios, and I think the notion of it being trendy to be after or beyond theory is being used as an excuse to neglect the responsibility to position one's work within a larger discourse. This would not be the case if postcriticality had been able to deliver some generative model for action and development, but it seems only to have been able to define that which it is not, which is this form of negation that seems to be always and only typified by references to Peter Eisenman. Instead of presenting new ideas, postcriticality has devolved into a reductive and totally banal idea about working with clients.

I attended a lecture you gave at the Berlage Institute in Rotterdam in 2006 which concluded with a discussion of the Pet Rock as a model for architecture that celebrates novelty, is inextricably tied to consumer desires, and stands for nothing in and of itself. I found this idea exciting in the midst of a bunch of angry, old-school Marxist European planning students, but Hickey's similar remarks, praising an intellectually vapid architectural practice to an American audience in the face of what appeared to be little to no agitation or protest, were disturbing. Now, I would be the last person to argue that innovative contemporary architecture must have some utopian social or political agenda in order to be worthwhile, but it should certainly have *some* agenda. Otherwise are we not just perpetuating the model of architecture as an increasingly marginalized service industry in which the vast majority of the profession operates and has always operated? What is your position on a worthwhile agenda for the profession? And what role do you assign to theorists like yourself in debates of this kind?

Sylvia Lavin— Thanks for your very interesting provocation. You seem to really get around, and it's fascinating to see how your mobility is linked to a keen sense that ideas and the discourses in which they are embedded are context-specific and sensitive to audience expectations. And indeed, therein lies one of the important and active contributions of the current post- (and you are correct, not to be confused with anti-) theoretical turn. Much of what once belonged to the domain of "theoretical" discovery was linked precisely to the role of the reader/audience/spectator in the production of meaning as well as to the institutional disciplines that made certain things possible to say and think while making other things impossible. Today, rather than expose the "fact" of this discursive structure, architects are instrumentalizing this hypothesis, using the variability of discourse to brand, market, persuade, explicate and otherwise move practices forward. Both Liz Diller and Alejandro Zaera-Polo, to name just two (and to pick them because Liz once typified the theoretical architect and Alejandro is sometimes used to exemplify the after-theoretical architect), have been explicit about their use of an expanded model of architectural discourse and the decisive role this capacity to speak in tongues has played in getting projects built, which I presume is at least one acceptable model of what it might mean to be "generative."

Discourse is only one arena in which the lessons of the theoretical era are being activated, expanding beyond their previous focus on the discipline and into questions of professional practice. Architects have hitherto had theory or shoptalk, but the building itself as well as the *realpolitik* of its production have generally been understood as resistant to theorization. The problem for us today is not the anti-theorists—there have always been and always will be plenty of those—the problem is how to reconstitute the modalities of practice as theorizable objects. For example, try to find nonessentializing or nonsemiotic means of thinking about materials and you will fail, or will need to invent them yourself. The brute isomorphism being established between moral rectitude and LEED certification is a phenomenon crying out for some theories of action sophisticated enough to get beyond the combined facts of professional guilt and personal appetite. And as for the *landscape uber alles* mantra, it makes me think of a fantastic short story by Leslie Dick about staying in a Neutra apartment, a hallmark of euphoric inside/outside/landscape living; she got bitten in the ass by a poisonous spider and almost died. Like most things, landscapes are good sometimes and not so good others: old theory can help you tell the difference and new theory can help you decide when to use which and where. You need both, and if you forget the former and embrace only the latter, watch your ass, since it will definitely become necrotic.

The disciplinary mobility of art critics is also a fascinating subject: so many of them these days are increasingly interested in architecture and design, but I suspect their tourism tells us more about the state of the art world than it does about architecture. When architecture critics stray into high art territories, they mostly get ignored, always the best defense, or fired from their jobs at prestigious New York City newspapers. But here too we can learn from old-school discourse analysis because art critics don't immediately become stupid when they get to architecture (although they often like to preface their remarks by saying things like, "well, I don't really know much about architecture and cannot read a plan"). Instead, it's important to understand that art critics remain art critics even when talking about buildings and in fact are talking to other art critics and to artists when they seem to be talking about architecture. They don't really analyze or read architecture but rather use buildings as a means to capture the attention of the vastly larger and broader audience that has become interested in architecture today and to smuggle into this milieu utopian aspirations that they reserve for art. In other words, art criticism needs architecture to function as the scapegoat for an impossible political and social mandate, in order to limit or at least define the demands that are made of art in the contemporary world. If architecture is invoked as that which is supposed to solve the problems of post-Katrina New Orleans, for example, architecture's inevitable failing sort of lets everyone else off the hook. The gambit (I'd call it a rhetorical gambit rather than a theory of architecture) distracts you from asking about what art or the general electorate, for that matter, is doing to change the social structures that made the apathy after

Katrina possible—apathy in this case being the most long-lasting form of devastation.

The models available to us for the active architect, for the architect of social consequence and political advancement, are indeed woefully inadequate. But the dumb and ill-educated architect, the one who doesn't know Mies or Derrida and still mistakes design for social policy, is not a good alternative. One role we can take on is not to mistake gambits for criticism. It's hard to imagine celebrating the fact that an artist made sure not to have too many ideas and to never let the few ideas they might have had get in their way. But making the same argument about architects is somehow plausible, even laudatory. Our acceptance of such assertions reveals the field's vulnerability and anxiety about its status in the world and its capacity to be the source for intelligence: its age-old anxiety that lurking behind every Latin text there remains a mason who cannot read. (I can't tell from your email if I am to suppose that what's wrong with architects is that they know some history or that they don't know enough or know the wrong history, so I don't know if I'm helping, sinning or simply stating the obvious when I note that Alberti defined the architect as a mason who had learned Latin.) Oh well, believing that using the color pink is enough for the professional practice of architecture to change the world is very sweet, and at least makes it a refreshing change from the dour sourness that had come to characterize the theoretical sensibility. But sweet or sour is not the point, unless you are at a Chinese restaurant. Instead, it's important to remember that architecture is not soup and it doesn't taste any better if Brad Pitt serves it to you.

BA— But really, to what extent are the likes of Liz Diller and Alejandro Zaero-Polo helping anybody make sense of the discipline's current state of ideological confusion? Doesn't this notion of speaking in tongues, at least in the work of FOA, ultimately boil down to lying about what your project is about in order to get a client to buy into it? And although Liz Diller might have once typified the theoretical architect, I find it difficult to discern how the level of critical speculation present in her early work has been expanded or evolved. She seems to have thrown it under the bus entirely as she started earning high-profile building projects and taking on more employees. By the time I was studying architecture and could hear her talk at Cooper Union, she was spending an hour and a half finger-pointing and complaining about how all of the content was being value-engineered out of her projects. It seems that the model here is less about being strategic with discourse to support some intelligent agenda than it is about getting work and still trying to look smart while you do it.

But maybe looking smart is as much as one can expect from practices like these today, and perhaps this would be enough if the kind of anxiety about taking definitive positions on the current relationship between theory and production did not seem to afflict academics just as much as it does prominent practitioners. I don't think you'll find much resistance to the assertion that the "modalities of practice" need to be theorized to empower architects to avoid nostalgia about materials or to challenge worn-out clichés about the relationship of architecture to landscape. I find it perhaps symptomatic of this condition that you would not, in your substantial response, take a specific position yourself on how to address problems like these collectively in relation to the scope of your own work, which seems to focus on a rigorous "theorization" of pop culture, or at least an attempt to enhance criticism by bridging it with contemporary problems of consumption, rather than either resisting or capitulating to them.

Matthew Allen

Control Yourself!
Lifestyle Curation in the Work of Sejima and Nishizawa

SANAA, Rolex Learning Center, EPFL,
Lausanne, Switzerland, 2009.

Although Kazuyo Sejima's projects have received nothing but praise since she began to practice in the early 1990s, this praise has been framed in terms of the most benign generalities. The discursive consensus that Sejima and her collaborator, Ryue Nishizawa, practice an unexceptional modernism has made it difficult to bring them into contemporary debates. While scathing criticism of Sejima and Nishizawa is hard to come by, frustrated readings are common. Alejandro Zaera-Polo's interview for *El Croquis* is typical.[1] In that interview, Zaera-Polo read into their work a deep concern with phenomenology and program that was systematically stifled by Sejima and Nishizawa's refusal to play along. While Zaera-Polo's projection of concerns did not entirely miss the mark, Sejima and Nishizawa's understated response represents a coherent position that cannot be easily subsumed by the typical architectural discourse which forms Zaera-Polo's theoretical milieu.

Sejima and Nishizawa's work is best characterized not by the formal qualities of transparency, blankness, minimalism, abstraction, and nonhierarchical programming that are surely present, but by how all of these attributes operate to make urban life a self-conscious aesthetic performance. Blankness calls for active projection, indeterminacy asks for participation, and the absence of spatial hierarchy requires communal initiative. Sejima and Nishizawa's projects for their collaborative international firm, SANAA, operate by curating a specific type of architectural subject. At the same time, inhabitants are encouraged by the architecture to aestheticize and curate their own lifestyle. "Curate" comes from the Latin *curare*, from which our term "care" derives. Sejima and Nishizawa's architecture cares for how people live their lives, but, more importantly, their architecture provokes people to care for their own lifestyle. This two-step curatorial logic is systematically projected onto all building types. Zollverein is a school in a white box; the Rolex Learning Center is a student center in an undulating white box; there are cafés, theaters, shops, and, of course,

museums in white boxes.[2] Each infuses its respective program with the atmosphere of a gallery, making everyday life a self-consciously aesthetic event.

Sejima and Nishizawa's curatorial logic has been best worked out in their recent housing projects. Housing is an obvious vehicle for a highly prescriptive project simply because people *choose* to live there; as long as demand for a type of housing exists in the market, developers can afford to defer the specifics of inhabitation to their architect. Residents can pick the impositions they like best. Sejima and Nishizawa's critical acclaim has given them great leeway. Their curatorial project is exhibited most clearly in Sejima's recently completed Seijo Townhouses because, just as with a well-run science experiment, a number of factors are controlled.[3] The project was designed for a somewhat unadventurous developer and made of an atypical material for Sejima: light pink brick.[4] Moriyama House—the canonical apartments-in-white-boxes project—deals with the same problems in a more ideal situation; it is important that it does not take the perfect client, site, and materials to achieve the desired effect. If Moriyama House was the first proof of a concept, the Seijo

1— Alejandro Zaera-Polo, "A Conversation," in *Kazuyo Sejima, 1983–2000 + Ryue Nishizawa, 1995–2000*, eds. Richard C. Levene and Fernando Márquez Cecilia (Barcelona: El Croquis, 2001), 8–21.

2— The Zollverein School and the Rolex Learning Center are projects by SANAA.

3— The Seijo Townhouses project is by Kazuyo Sejima & Associates, Sejima's sole proprietorship.

4— Cathelijne Nuijsink, "Beneath the Surface," *Mark* 13 (April/May 2008): 105.

Townhouses project is evidence of its pervasive application in Sejima and Nishizawa's work.

At first glance the plans of Seijo Townhouses seem typically Miesian. Only the loose organization of the alternating orthogonal buildings and courtyard spaces distinguish these designs from Mies's courtyard house project of 1934. The section reveals that the small, box-like volumes above ground are the result of placing larger programmatic elements in the basement, admittedly a concession made to the developer and the housing market. The elevations, rhythmic alternations of overlapping short, medium, and tall boxes, share a common language with many other Sejima and Nishizawa projects. Abstract white planes are punctured by large picture windows. The visual effect is to create a playful village: a cartoon of housing. Fourteen apartments deceptively occupy twenty small, seemingly disconnected buildings (which are in fact all connected at the basement level). So far—looking only at plans, sections, and elevations—the central concerns of the Seijo Townhouses remain invisible, hidden behind a convincing formal logic.

Then one comes across interviews with Sejima describing the project. She starts off with the simplest and most banal of explanations: "most importantly," she says, "I tried to make a good living environment for fourteen families in one complex."[5] This meant providing "proximity to greenery and soil ... light and wind from two or more directions ... [and] views in various directions as well." Then she becomes more specific: "residents," Sejima says, "are responsible for creating a good living environment.... Some of the communal space belongs to your neighbor, while at another place it's as though you, as resident, get part of that communal space back." Then finally a confession: "I tried to make housing in which living isn't as easy as it might be."[6]

Looking at the photographs of the project, we get a sense of what this not-so-easy living entails. The photographs show the projection of a self-consciously disciplined, aestheticized lifestyle onto the domestic

environment. The architecture itself demands that its inhabitants undertake this curation. In a typical view of a representative space, we see a white room with a picture window—with desk, potted plants, and chair—looking over a sparse, manicured garden. Through a similar picture window in an abstract wall-plane, we glimpse across into another white box with table, chairs, and potted plants. Two families, urban, educated, and upper middle class, overlook each other. The room in the foreground is an inhabited gallery space. The two picture windows frame another, similar gallery. While modernism has traditionally idealized the home as a container of art—caricatured by Adolf Loos in "The Poor Little Rich Man" and definitively instantiated in Philip Johnson's Glass House—the very privacy of modernist domesticity precluded the recognition of gallery *culture* at the center of a common social system. The reciprocal surveillance of Seijo requires the building's inhabitants to curate their own lifestyle. Rather than the omnipresent surveillance of Foucaultian disciplinary societies, Seijo exhibits the "free-floating control" described by Deleuze as the late-twentieth-century successor to Foucault's

5— Ibid., 106–108.
6— Ibid.

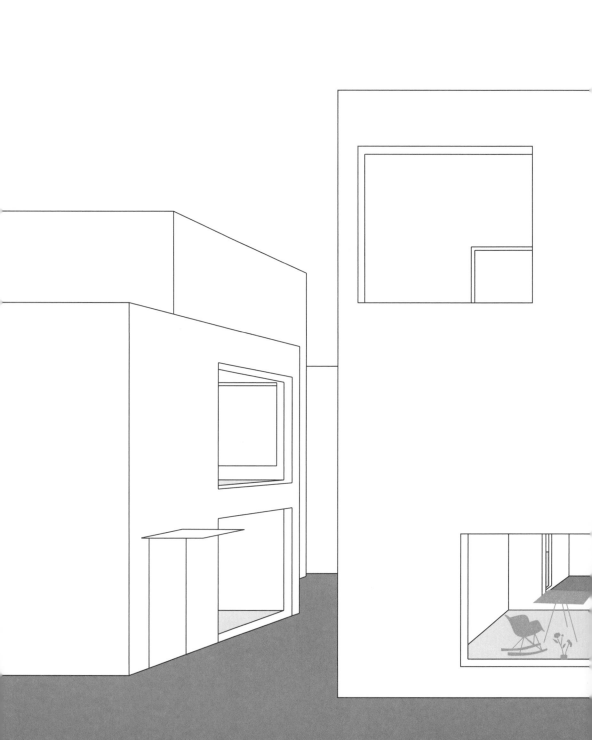

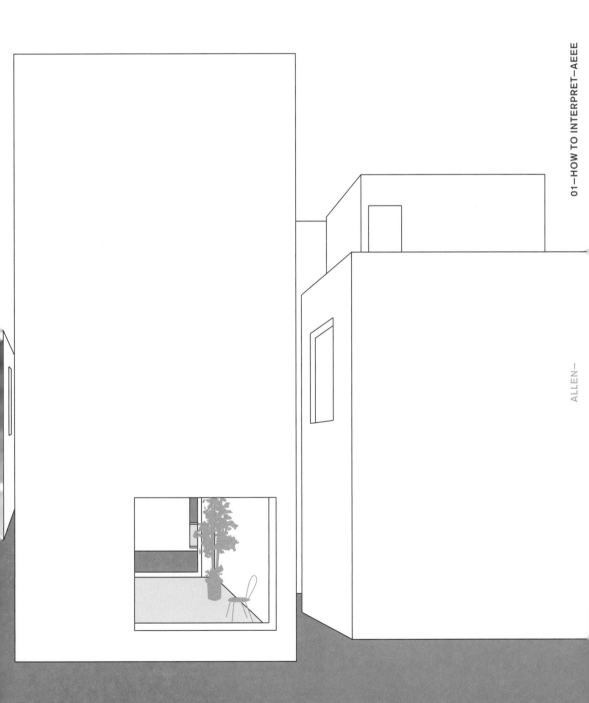

ALLEN—

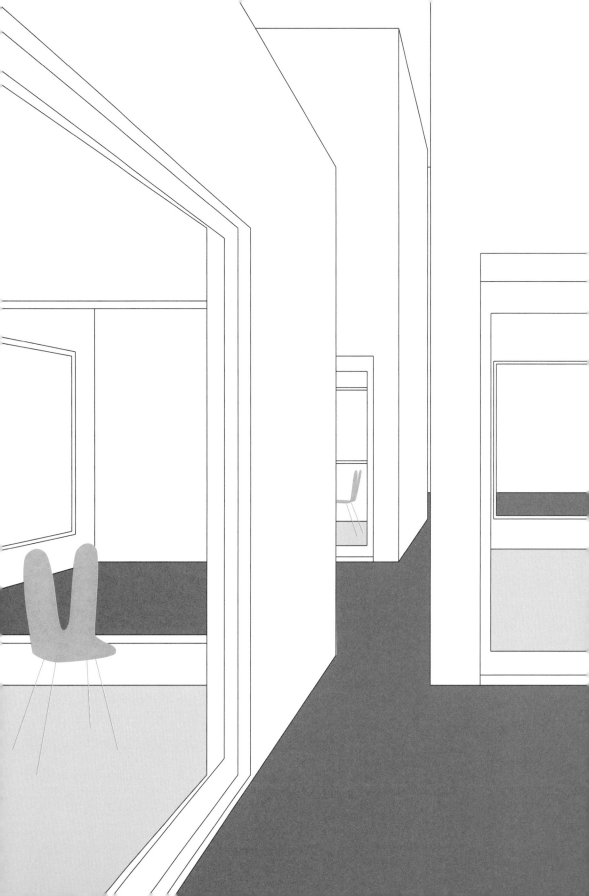

nineteenth-century paradigm. By "motivating" inhabitants to "modulate" their inhabitation of their own home, Seijo is the archetype of housing in the "society of control."[7] Inhabitants regulate their own behavior not as a response to a disciplinary authority, but as a way to fit within a socially determined aesthetic of life.

Insisting that residents pay attention to the aesthetic details of their daily life is a steep price for a luxury condo. But this is the central allure of Sejima and Nishizawa's work; it contains a crucial political insight. In explaining why the Russian people were not making good revolutionaries in the aftermath of the establishment of the Soviet Union, Leon Trotsky complained that Russians lack the habit of deliberate attention to detail characteristic of other societies. In those weeks of civil war and mass revelry, Russians proved they would rather give their lives for the revolution than clean their rifles or polish their boots. But without creating self-disciplined order in everyday life, the military and political gains made by the proletariat were sure to erode. The revolution, rather than being a public political event, was a matter of lifestyle.[8]

The curation of a self-disciplined lifestyle: it is hard to believe that white walls and picture windows could be responsible for so much. In assessing the New Museum for *Log*, Kurt Forster opined that "when no historical baggage weighs down the flight of the architect's imagination, we might expect more than a return to the familiar 'white cube.'"[9] He finds in the end, however, that "the authority of the New Museum evolves from the 'blank,' from its power to still and allay the very force that resides in works of art. As a result, the museum exercises its authority by dint of its *extinguishing power*, sapping as it were the residual life vested in the works of art that find their way under its roof."[10] His analysis ought to have gone on to explore how this power is reinvested in museumgoers, but for a museum this would not be an out-of-the-ordinary occurrence. Michael Fried argued long ago that the entire project of minimalism was to make art mute so that art-viewing could become a self-reflexive performance.[11] Sejima and Nishizawa's innovation is to use the atmosphere typical of a gallery in the architecture of housing, offices, theaters, cafés, shops, game parlors, and the like. While other architecture might elaborate walls, interiors, windows, and gardens as figures in their own right, Sejima and Nishizawa leave these elements blank. As a result, the attention of inhabitants shifts to the aesthetic performance of their inhabitation.

It is surprising that Sejima and Nishizawa have found so many projects in which to develop this agenda of turning lifestyles into works of art; this is perhaps proof that they have hit upon a general cultural condition at the turn of the century. Photographs of the post inhabitation Moriyama House show image-conscious young architects and eccentric professionals whose lifestyle involves meticulously crafted social spectacle. In the New Museum, New York aesthetes at openings make aesthetic discipline look easy. But even in the much more difficult case of a large office building—such as SANAA's Novartis campus—the view out a window, through a courtyard, and into a blank space on the other side somehow creates the distance and staging necessary for the atmosphere of a gallery. Office work, against all odds, becomes art.

7— Gilles Deleuze, "Postscript on the Societies of Control," *October* 59 (Winter 1992): 3–7.

8— Isaac Deutscher, *The Prophet Armed* (New York: Verso, 2003), 266.

9— Kurt Forster, "The New Museum in New York: A Whitewash?" *Log* 12 (Spring/Summer 2008): 6.

10— Ibid., 12.

11— Michael Fried, *Art and Objecthood: Essays and Reviews* (Chicago: University of Chicago Press, 1998), 148–172.

The atmosphere of the gallery has been steadily evolving since the Renaissance. In the late nineteenth century, John Ruskin advocated the use of museums as an "example of perfect order and perfect elegance ... to the disorderly and rude populace."[12] As museums have oscillated between populist and elitist agendas and cultural capital has taken on ever more nuanced forms, this agenda has been subtly tweaked. Andrea Fraser has identified the "museum's purpose as not only to publicize art, but to publicize art as an emblem of bourgeois privacy. Its purpose, in a sense, is to publicize privacy. It is in this, it would seem, that the museum's educational function consists."[13] Sejima and Nishizawa's work short-circuits Fraser's formula, instituting the gallery in all spheres of privacy (there is no longer a public sphere, after all). In their hands, architecture becomes a device of self-education.

The contemporary culture of self-discipline has been interpreted as a long resurgence of social conservatism after a short period of radical experimentation; this was Deleuze's conclusion in his "Postscript on the Societies of Control." While the present is certainly the opposite of the sixties, the flip has been not from radical to conservative, but from a culture of optimism to a culture of realism. Sejima and Nishizawa's unwillingness to exaggerate their own agenda is a sign that the agency of political change has shifted from the sweeping gesture of theory to the subtlety of ethics. Theory is premised

12— John Ruskin, *The Works of John Ruskin*, eds. E. T. Cook and A. Wedderburn, 39 vols. (London: Geo. Allen), vol. 30 (1907), 53; vol. 34 (1908), 247; quoted in Andrew McClellan, "A Brief History of The Art Museum Public," in *Art and its Publics: Museum Studies at the Millenium*, ed. Andrew McClellan (Malden; MA: Blackwell Publishing Ltd., 2003), 8.

13— Andrea Fraser, "Notes on the Museum's Publicity," in *Museum Highlights: The Writings of Andrea Fraser*, ed. Alexander Alberro (Cambridge: MIT Press, 2005), 92.

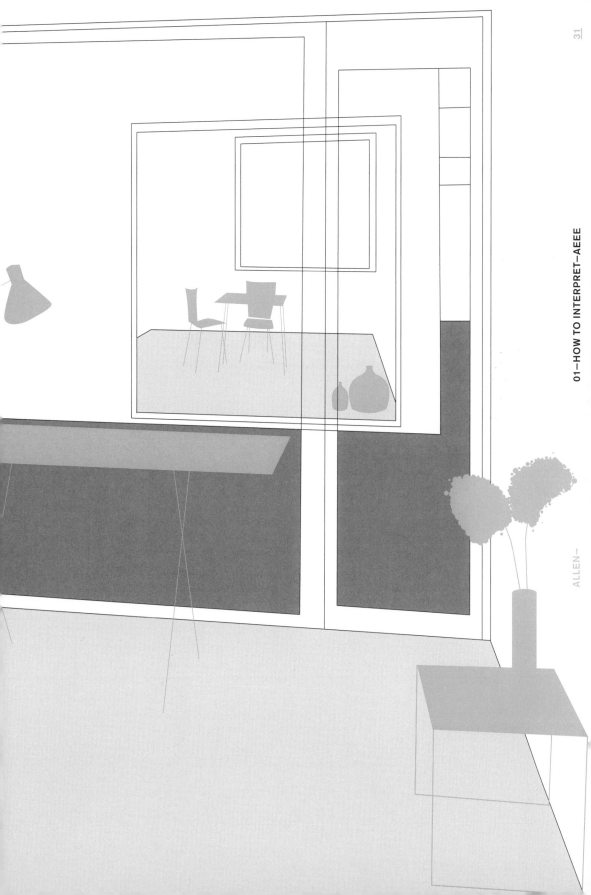

on the belief that culture is subject to critique by someone in the position to grasp its deep contradictions—a broad agenda for an optimistic time. The realist agenda of ethics limits its scope to, as Foucault put it, the "technologies of the self."[14] Slavoj Žižek has been the most vocal enumerator of the differences between critique and self-discipline. It is easy, he says, to condemn Lenin (for example, but also the Red Guards, the Taliban, et alia), but the fact that his worldview was articulated in his micropolitical actions means there is something we can learn from the way Lenin lived his life, quite apart from more sweeping moral issues.[15] Developing an ethics through architecture—what I have been calling curating a lifestyle—is a small goal when compared to the social transformation promised by critique, but it is perhaps more realistic.

Extrapolating from the work of Sejima and Nishizawa, then, and taking Trotsky's call for self-discipline as the foundation of politics, we can imagine an architecture that is not critical of its social context, but instead shifts speculation to finding ways of isolating, reinforcing, and foregrounding existing forms of self-consciousness while playing down any architectural concept that might get in the way. The problem becomes how to understate architecture in order to curate specific and already-existing lifestyles. If the New Museum traps and extinguishes art for the sake of the museumgoers' edification, and the Seijo Townhouses make life difficult and deliberate in order to create community, what other micropolitical moments can the architect curate? What architecture does it take to make a given lifestyle distinct and self-conscious? The same gallery does not work for all situations, but Sejima and Nishizawa have shown that the generalizable function of the gallery is a powerful device with which to aestheticize life.

14— Michel Foucault, "Technologies of the Self," in Technologies of the Self: A Seminar with Michel Foucault, eds. Luther H. Martin, Patrick H. Hutton, and Huck Gutman (Amherst: University of Massachusetts Press, 1988),16–49.

15— See Slavoj Žižek, In Defense of Lost Causes (New York: Verso, 2008), and Slavoj Žižek, "Afterword: Lenin's Choice," in Vladimir Il'ich Lenin, Revolution at the Gates: A Selection of Writings from February to October, 1917, ed. Slavoj Žižek (New York: Verso, 2002), 165–336.

01–HOW TO INTERPRET–AEEE

ALLEN–

Kazuyo Sejima & Associates, Seijo Townhouses, Tokyo, Japan, 2007.

Critical
Conditions——
A conversation between Liam Gillick and Michael Meredith

Michael Meredith— Rosalind Krauss, writing of structural-
ist film and poststructuralist video, has commented:
"the specificity of mediums, even modernist ones, must
be understood as differential, self-differing, and thus
as a layering of conventions never simply collapsed into
the physicality of their support.... It is precisely the
onset of higher orders of technology...which allow us, by
rendering older techniques outmoded, to grasp the inner
complexity of the mediums those
techniques support."[1] It seems that
your work has consistently used one
medium—say, a book—to comment on
another, such as an installation.
I was wondering how you would characterize your use of various media.
What would you say to the claim that
we are in a postmedium condition?
Do you consider yours a postmedium
art practice?

1— Rosalind Krauss,
*"A Voyage on the North
Sea": Art in the Age
of the Post-Medium
Condition* (New York:
Thames and Hudson
Inc., 1999), 53.

Liam Gillick— In some ways, I certainly accept her
statement. It is an art historian's statement connected
to the particular history of American late-modernist
practice, one that is embedded in attempting to understand "choices" and working out why someone might do
something and use a particular medium for it. But while
the statement is valid, it does not account for the contingency of materials and the specificities of material
relationships in various contexts. I am not postmedium,
nor does my work follow or make the claims that Krauss
indicates. I am sure she would agree that there are artists who both acknowledge the potential of her statement
and deny it simultaneously.

I am more interested in notions of production and the
specific contexts of production. A focus on techniques
and materials is an art historical obsession. It tells
you very little about *why* things are made, *by whom* and
for whom. Rather than abstractly questioning how a material or a technology feeds into the other, I find it more
interesting to examine how these media are chosen and
worked with in the first place. The contingent quality of
choices does not result in a "balance" between intention
and results. Instead, this contingency creates productive
spaces between artistic or architectural intentionality
and the conditions of production. There are economic,
psychological and political factors. The search for new
technological solutions that might function as indicators
of the desire to align with the new so often produces

merely apparently new methods that do nothing of the
sort. There is no clear, resolvable relationship between
intentions and the conditions of production.

What happens in my work is that I am radically
inconsistent (which is not the same as being radical
or inconsistent) about the starting point of any specific project. Some things are determined by context,
others by the desire to enter into new material relationships, and others by the aim to just get something
out as quickly as possible to make a point. Terms
such as "postmedium" are not enough to explain this
increasingly common working methodology.

> <u>MM</u>— We [at MOS] see our practice as postmedium. Since
> it is composed of drawings, diagrams and sketches, with
> or without convention, in addition to "real" constructed
> objects, architecture is inherently representational.
> The practice of architecture, as opposed to build-
> ing, is already highly mediated and discursive, and
> therefore there *is* a relationship between intention and
> representation, understanding that representation is
> architectural production. The goal of architecture as
> a discipline is to both produce and reflect ideas of
> cultural progress through representation. This is an
> important distinction between architecture and art. If
> you're a painter, you are working directly with a clear
> understanding of the medium of paint; even as a painter
> when you work in video, you are still talking about
> painting. In architecture, by contrast, we rarely actu-
> ally build the thing that we are designing, and conse-
> quently representation itself becomes our inherently
> unstable, post-medium medium.
>
> Today, the idea of architecture has been expanded to the
> point that it's not necessarily about the specifics of
> construction. In fact, we know from previous avant-garde
> models (think: Peter Eisenman) that architecture can be
> divorced from materiality, and that "form" can be pitted
> against "material." The result of that model was that the
> discursive aspect of architecture became highly and per-
> haps overly charged even within itself. In architecture,
> the avant-garde is always a representational project. Our
> generation of architects is seen as the "practice" gen-
> eration that tries to escape representation by actually
> building and engaging with the real (material) world.
> But at the same time, our office is trying to rethink
> the avant-garde representational project. We propose
> an architecture which operates on multiple registers by
> both expanding the real and material into the realm of

fiction, and constructing fictions as well as facts. We
are subverting the dialectic opposition between pragma-
tists and utopians because this construct is no longer
useful. In our studio, we don't necessarily make buildings; right now we are making movies.

One of the roles of architecture is to produce new subjectivities—new ways of thinking and talking and looking—
and our approach is to blur and transgress the boundary
between material and ideal until utopian projects start
popping up in the space of the pragmatic. In this way, we
are interested in producing things that are difficult to
classify. They work as weird or "sublime" ideas removed
from their referents; they are disturbing because one
doesn't know yet how to think about them. I have always
seen your work running on a similar track. It seems you
are trying to produce a sort of local sublime (in the
sense of Rancière's reworking of Lyotard) that collapses
the construction of opposition between autonomy and het-
eronomy in much the same way.

LG— Yes. Like you, I work to achieve this with con-
sciously pragmatic techniques. I use the "screen" as both
a creative medium itself and the way to subsequently connect context and production. I am not working or thinking alone when I produce something for a specific context
because there are others involved in the dialogue. The
result of this multipronged conversation is the production of a specific medium or set of media for a particular situation and particular agents. The "local sublime"
of social relationships becomes my medium. These interactions, in turn, motivate the selection of material,
functions, location, et cetera. I always think in relation to material facts, meaning I don't ever think of
an "effect" or an "idea" and then try to find a way of
expressing that with a material choice. Regardless of
Peter Eisenman's efforts within the discourse of architecture, I hold that materials and ideas are linked
absolutely. Because of this, I use forms and materials
that have an existing function and set of associations in
the world in a way that demands participation. I see this
way of working as representing the real negotiations of
the everyday in terms of a practice that needs to find a
form, a material and a site.

Architecture (as larger and smaller than building) is
different. There has been an exchange of terminology
between art and architecture. Architecture has absorbed
the "language of creativity," muddling the organic, the
technological and the legacy of late-modernist formalism.

The way someone might describe a material or structural
decision is couched in what I can only describe as the
language of creativity ex nihilo. As an example, the most
recent architect I worked with was absorbed with pushing
me to "talk through" material choices and "explain color
choices." My work is more pragmatic than this. It relates
to real preexisting conditions and explains the web of
relationships around these conditions. Architecture has
to reach beyond that, but do so with a consciousness of
the problems created when you "reach beyond."

MM— Architecture is more interesting than art for me,
because we have clients and because we intervene in complex situations. We have more characters participating in
architecture; relational aesthetics is inherently a part
of what we do. We have to take part in a highly charged
set of constituencies, including clients and socioeconomic issues. Sustainability and mechanical systems and
the needs of clients make the pursuit of the ontological
experiments of architecture interesting and relevant;
they are part of the project of bringing new constituencies into the conversation of architecture.

And architecture is one of those discursive practices
that empower generational struggle. We need to be able to
transform or destroy systems and techniques which come
before us. For better or worse, culture and humanity need
to constantly produce new spaces for new experiments, and
architecture is able to destabilize the past in order to
produce these spaces.

But having said that, art trumps architecture in one
important way. I think producing newness in terms of
novel forms and effects in order to enfranchise a con-
stituency is noble, important and deeply social, and art
is simply a better vehicle for this activity. In architecture, the problem is that these effects are temporary
and ephemeral, while architecture (even today) is not.
When architecture is built, it requires the expenditure
of all kinds of things at a significant scale, and once
its effects are absorbed, its cultural impact is already
history. These architectural tchotchkes become part of
the junk of the world. They keep us moving in new directions, but they litter the planet. Sometimes it seems
that architects produce entropy in the name of order.
Nevertheless, I'd rather invent the novel thing that
eventually becomes an anachronism than the functional
object that has no cultural impact.

LG— This is a simple difference between art and design. Design does not become art when it is expensive and unique; it just becomes expensive and unique. I aim to produce newness not in terms of objects, but rather in terms of contingencies and relationships. I am interested in the semiotics of the built world. I accept that I operate within existing structures. Therefore, I have to find a way to unsettle or intervene within these structures. This preference on the part of some architects for producing what is called an "interesting solution" can interfere with acknowledging the inescapable condition of intervening in the real world. Contingent work has come under fire from those who believe in autonomy via refusal: from those who believe that the role of art or architecture is to teach or document above and beyond its direct supersubjective operation. But, as you said, architecture is relational by definition, precisely because of the way in which architecture is produced over and above the way that architecture (as objects and theory) acts. The distinction is important. Deploying "creative" language about playing with materials and surfaces and solutions is not discourse; it is the opposite of discourse. Discourse in a developed sense accounts for the languages within the conversation, including a self-consciousness about description: a politics of describing. The best architects change the language of doing something. But the "system" doesn't really want this, so there is a strong pressure to absorb real innovation and concrete changes in society by separating out the terms used to describe material relationships from the actual function and potential of a structure.

There is a strong self-interest in architecture to be incomplete ... it is the only way it can survive. Every built project has its moments of crisis in relation to how things actually get built and who gets to build them, and these moments are used to create space for the different actors in the project. The most successful commercial architects are deft at withholding and leaving spaces of indecision within an ambience of precise decision-making. It is within these gaps that they get to move on to the next project. This crisis of incompletion, which is by definition embedded in architectural strategy, is much more productive than the art context.

MM— But I don't think meaning is inherently attached to architectural activity. I think we construct narratives about forms, effects, uses, all the different parts of architecture, and that these narratives are critical or not critical in terms of the position they construct toward the status quo. The same object will seem critical at one moment and not at another. For instance, Peter Eisenman's grid was a critical apparatus; now it is banal iconography. Nevertheless, it remains important for avant-garde architects to think of new forms of counter-intuitive noise to be deployed in existing networks. For our office, this means bringing humor and lightness back into architecture, and destroying the previous tragic construction of architectural imagination, which always sorted things out into hyperbolic dialectics. I think the usefulness of opposition is over and we have to bring something new (or something old) into play: contradiction, surprise, absurdity. We have to recapture and reemploy the referential qualities of architecture. We have to recycle some of the lessons of Venturi or learn to operate like Warhol after abstract expressionism.

In this way we negate a certain evaluation of architecture which framed it in anxiety and heaviness—not in order to throw away history, but in order to clear a space of ground for new critical endeavors. We have to come to grips with the fact that pure negation itself is a myth, and it also has to be negated, so we are deploying the myth of negation or "antidesign" to demythologize the demythologized myth, so to speak. In being critical of architecture through architecture, we also create the space from which to project new ontologies and new ways of seeing and understanding into the world. This is inevitably a failed project at some level precisely because it is temporal. At some point you realize it is going to end badly, that you will be the old guy wearing bell-bottoms one day. But in the meantime, the repetitive erasure accomplished by critical architecture, however it is defined by each successive generation, creates socially powerful fictions. Erasing is not starting over: it's Rauschenberg erasing de Kooning, or superimposing so many references on the existing that the original is obliterated. Architecture enfranchises people in the same way that a definitive album can enfranchise a generation. Architecture is always creating new narratives to spur those who feel the need to clear a little space for themselves in the wild mess of the world.

LG— My art is not about creating or spurring narratives but instead about acting in response to the spurs and conflicts in the existing tangle of relationships. They asked Žižek to become a culture minister and he said no, but I wouldn't mind being the finance minister.... My interests are in systems rather than icons, at either the scale of art or the scale of architecture. At the moment, my work is quite pragmatic and deals with renovation, discussion and projection. It does not lend itself well to the creation of a total form. It operates under the regime of architecture, but it is not architecture. It is at the interface between art and the pragmatic architecture of the built world.

I am, however, beginning to feel that I may have come to the limit of intervention, partly because I am increasingly being invited to work alongside "urban renewal" projects and I find the process of dealing with all the interested parties problematic. The hardcore corruption involved in getting things built at the architectural scale is one thing that's holding me back from doing "pure architecture." I did one small renovation in Belgium for an affordable housing project, but it was an enormous fight and I was floored by the unethical practices of the city's representatives. But it is something I want to go further with.

MM— It's important not to confuse architecture with building. For me (and for architectural discourse), not all buildings are architecture. Architecture includes buildings elevated to enable discussion, scrutiny and value. This is the autonomous part of the discipline. Architects and those who care about architecture assign this value in a fraught, collective way. We are constantly reevaluating what architecture is, and this evolving valuation is the shared process of art and architecture. Of course our decisions are affected by the world and by the input of indifferent and uninterested people, but I still believe that schools, publishers, students, practitioners, museums, et cetera, are all responsible together for determining what we think of as architecture. Either we have to agree that all buildings are architecture (which we don't) or we have to agree that evaluation of them is part of the disciplinary terrain itself. Personally, I'm not interested in *everything* being architecture because it means there is no political discourse, and the politics of definition are crucial. History is defined by the shifts—from geometry to form and to use—in how we assign value to architecture. As architects, we don't all sit around thinking about drop ceilings and technical details. We are really thinking about the work as it relates to other work. We are thinking about instrumentality and agency. All projects of architecture (and art) are essentially historical,

and architecture is inherently a generational construct
that is shifting and reactionary. My biggest problem at
the moment, and I think you would agree, is that the baby
boomers have a stranglehold on the evaluation of actions
and objects. They have made evaluations and disciplinary
definitions seem stable, when in fact they are not.

LG— I agree. I am not "postdisciplinary" any more than
I am postmedium. I operate within an art context. Even
though you can make something for a gallery and I can
come up with a new entry phone system for a public housing project, you remain within the context of architecture and I remain within art. After Duchamp, any activity
that a self-nominated artist takes on is already art by
intention, and this has nothing to do with reception.
Architecture also has its disciplinary boundary, regardless of artists who label themselves architects. Most
post-studio artists adopt the stylistic trappings of a
fantasy of the architect's "office"—myself included, up
to a point. Vito Acconci actually calls himself an architect, but he is technically breaking a law if he does
this in certain states.... I, on the other hand, conspire
with architects in the renomination of spaces to make use
of the copyright and moral-right protections that are
afforded to artists and their work.

MM— Vito is breaking the law in *every* state. The discipline's idea of an architect is someone who is participating in the conversation with architects. Vito is
talking to artists. There has to be some social consensus that Vito is an architect in order for him to become
important to the architectural discourse. One side of
architecture is a highly legal, liable profession. We are
responsible for the life safety of people; we have this
serious burden of making sure that we are not killing
people, and that if there's a fire, they can get out and
if there's a storm, the building will stand up. This is
hardcore social responsibility.

LG— Yes. My entry phone system is a decision by an artist to take over a terrain that expects an artist to
offer a "design solution" that will improve "the quality of life" in some abstract way, by instead producing
a practical system. Your decision to make something for
a gallery is an acknowledgement that an architect's work
needs to be seen under the critical conditions of art
production. The question is one of social and political
expectation. The discussion is necessarily elusive if
you merely look at the relationship between intention and
physical function, because there is a historically unique

proximity between art and architecture that transcends certainties. The nature of the respective practices is that the boundary gets moved all the time. Just when you think you have reached it, you will find it has shifted somewhere else. There is a dialogue that is real, but it takes place within a necessary and functional, mutable boundary. Without this boundary, there would be no dialectical potential, let alone discursive potential. But in order to find an effective way to work within this, you might need to think of what Nanni Moretti says near the beginning of *Caro Diario*: "Even in a society more decent than this one, I will only feel in tune with a minority of people. I believe in people but I just don't believe in the majority of people. I will always be in tune with a minority of people."[2]

This is easy for an artist to say and hard for an architect to justify. Maybe somewhere here we find a space to actually find real antagonism and difference rather than just questions of taste or manners.

2— *Caro Diario*, directed by Nanni Moretti, with Nanni Moretti (Sacher Films, 1993).

Douglas Wu

Metaphoric Architecture

The National Grand Theater, designed by French architect Paul Andreu and completed in 2008, was the first of a host of recent landmarks by renowned western architects in China. Although it aimed to be Beijing's answer to the Sydney Opera House, its ultra-abstract form, known by the city as the "Egg," sparked national outrage over the architect's perceived disregard for the city's surrounding context and culture. Criticism of the National Theater focused not on the abstract design itself, but on its contextual relationship and placement within Beijing's historic and cultural center, across from the Forbidden City and the adjacent Tiananmen Square. Critics labeled the design introverted, insensitive and arrogant, and accused it of ignoring any reference to the history and tradition of China.[1] As more foreign star-architects experimented with high-budget architectural commissions, the backlash toward these new forms compelled the Chinese government to reexamine its position on architectural development.

1— Michael Hammond, "Paul Andreu's Beijing Grand Theatre Stirs the Dragon," *World Architecture News*, 2007, http://www.world architecturenews.com/index. php?fuseaction=wanappln. commentview&comment_ id=67 (accessed February 19, 2009).

Paul Andreu, The National Grand Theater, Beijing, China, 2007.

Herzog and de Meuron, Beijing National
Stadium, Beijing, China, 2008.

Through this process, two critical issues in contemporary Chinese architecture emerged. The first is the country's general lack of direction in architectural design. With few resources for research and development in the past fifty years, China has slowly been emerging from a design vacuum. The second is western architects' slow recognition of China's deep tradition of weaving metaphors and symbolism into its forms of cultural edification. This approach continues to affect the perception of architecture and the manner in which buildings are designed within China, and it is my focus here. Despite recent criticism that has dismissed metaphoric

architecture as shallow and imitative,[2] the cultural phenomenon of metaphorism can be framed as a positive maneuver in Chinese architecture because it extends the potential for a contemporary critical regionalism while providing a culturally sensitive and multivalent direction for the practice.

For almost three decades, China has pursued two major design directions: the first imported western styles of modern and postmodern architecture, which were often adapted to suit local (and therefore more economical) construction materials and techniques, while the second engaged in a revivalist interpretation of traditional historic

architecture, using modern materials in imitation of ancient motifs. Although the first direction has always been met with hostility from local audiences, the second strategy illustrates how China's early attempts at infusing modern architecture with its own culture have proven equally problematic. Architects, usually at the request of developers or government bureaucrats, attempted to reference vernacular styles by literally transplanting elements representative of Chinese historic architecture onto modernist boxes. The practice of planting the large, upturned roofs from traditional temples atop plain concrete buildings, for instance, became known as the "Big-Hat" style. For a period, Big-Hat was even mandated by the mayor of Beijing as a requirement for the city's newly constructed buildings, in an attempt to form a "Chinese" cityscape.[3] This kind of verbatim referencing, however, has not been limited to architecture of the past. The design language for significant buildings in China today has merely shifted from the explicit incorporation of historic architectural elements to the equally explicit incorporation of symbolic objects. Shanghai's Oriental Pearl Tower is a case in point: its architects illustrated China's colonial moniker as the "Pearl of the Orient" by mounting an actual giant sphere on the top of a tower. Both tactics of direct referencing fail to reinterpret symbols in an *architectural* context. More successfully, Herzog and de Meuron's Beijing National Stadium employed abstract architectural form as a vehicle for cultural connections. The metaphoric quality of the "Bird's Nest," as it became known, symbolized the strong Chinese emphasis on family unity while presenting a formally and structurally striking example of architecture.[4] HdeM's integration of facade, structure and meaning into a unified metaphoric package created an

2— See Sylvia Lavin, "Practice Makes Perfect," *Hunch: The Berlage Institute Report,* no. 11 (Winter 2006/2007): 106–113.

3— Lawrence Liauw, "Urbanization of Post-Olympic Beijing," *306090* 13 (2008): 215–221.

4— Although Swiss architects Herzog and de Meuron designed the Bird's Nest, the concept received considerable conceptual input from noted Chinese artist Ai Wei Wei.

impact which extended beyond architectural discourse and into the city's social fabric; the design won unanimous recognition from both design critics and the general public.

In China, metaphors and symbolism are not mere imagery, applied on the surface of things; instead, their architectural deployment offers a two-fold strategy that has the power to negotiate between modern forms and ancient cultural contexts. This hybridity of effect emerges out of the interaction between traditional concepts and contemporary situations, where traditional concepts are not simply applied to the new, but rather supply the framework through which novel conditions are to be understood. As Donald Schön has discussed, this "displacement" allows traditional concepts themselves to be seen in new ways "in order to function as projective models" for present circumstances.[5] In the Chinese context, the Bird's Nest offers an evolutionary possibility that displaces literal referencing in favor of more sophisticated intermeshings between contemporaneity and history.

Horse Character Evolution

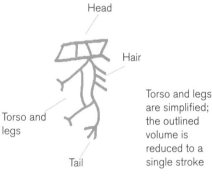

Head

Hair

Torso and legs

Tail

Torso and legs are simplified; the outlined volume is reduced to a single stroke

Eye becomes representative of head

Hair

Tail is enlarged

Leg and head are represented by single continuous stroke— character evolves into a writing system instead of a custom-made representation of an object

Head is abstracted into a few connec strokes

Tail is enlarged to become a volume-defining component

Like all developments that are legible to a public the moment they appear in a particular context, this hybrid approach can be traced back to the foundations of the culture in question. Engrained in Chinese ways of understanding and inhabiting the world is a large ensemble of metaphors that function as a set of shared moral values; these metaphors are instilled not through direct reference but through *inference*.[6] Traditional Chinese ink paintings, for example, are collections of broad but precisely related brush strokes.

Each stroke collaborates with its adjacent markings to create fields of intensity that may culminate to form identifiable objects such as a mountain, fish or bird. This occurs not through exact depiction, but by conforming to existing codes which accumulate *to imply* an image already captured within a shared cultural repertoire. The implied image is valued as both a symbol and an allusion; these work in tandem to imbue the art with layers of depth and meaning. In this way, the full meaning(s) of traditional Chinese paintings must be

5— Donald Schön, *Displacement of Concepts* (London: Tavistock Publications Limited, 1963), 192. Quoted in Chris Abel, *Architecture and Identity: Responses to Cultural and Technological Change* (Oxford: Oxford University Press, 1992), 103.

6—Alan Holgate, *Aesthetics of Built Form* (Oxford: Oxford University Press, 1992), 38.

Overall form achieves sense of upright directionality

Strokes become more directional, deliberate and defined

Original head and torso become generalized into single system of standardized vertical and horizontal strokes

Original legs are abstracted into standardized components of short strokes

Definition of form and volume is achieved; outline replaces hatch stroke and returns to earliest method (loss of historical process)

Original legs are abstracted further

interpreted or imagined by a viewer conversant in metaphor; the formal suggestiveness of the image is only the first and most apparent of multiple significations.

The most compelling argument for the central importance of metaphors in Chinese culture can be located in the written Chinese language itself. The Chinese character system is based on an evolution from pictorial representation to abstracted and compound symbols. This process, whereby an image of a tree becomes a diagram and then, in turn, a symbol that stands for a tree, is the basis for the way the Chinese learn to read and write; complex characters are traced back to representation. As the Chinese written language operates through symbols which not only stand for but also enact objects, the very practice of literacy informs the Chinese connection to culture through metaphors.

The possible architectural implications of this cultural location of meaning within

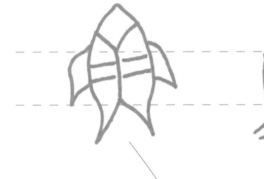

Fish Character Evolution

Multiple curves of the head are replaced by diagonal strokes— a strategy to define spatial quality through representative lines, while moving away from formal imitation

Tail fin simplified

Tail fin is standardized, but most importantly, its separation from main body compartmentalizes the parts, demonstrating a willingness to go beyond an adherence to phyisical form metaphor are worth exploring in some depth. The metaphoric qualities of architecture in China, developing from crude to more successful explorations, can be studied through a comparison with the evolution of the Chinese written character. Every major evolutionary phase of the Chinese character, or *hanzi*, represented a significant step away from imitative pictographic forms and toward an abstracted symbol. As the *hanzi* shed its pictorial qualities in favor of a more sophisticated written

form, metaphoric architecture should learn to allude without mimicry. To project how this process might happen, I will compare three existing buildings with three stages of Chinese characters: "Oracle Bone Inscription," "Small Seal Script," and "Standard Square Script." The buildings were all designed within the past five years, and they are each meant as metaphorical allusions to the dragon, which is one of China's strongest cultural references.

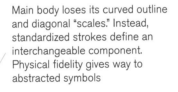

Main body loses its curved outline and diagonal "scales." Instead, standardized strokes define an interchangeable component. Physical fidelity gives way to abstracted symbols

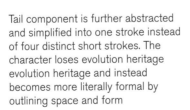

Tail component is further abstracted and simplified into one stroke instead of four distinct short strokes. The character loses evolution heritage evolution heritage and instead becomes more literally formal by outlining space and form

Car Character Evolution
(From Cart to Automobile)

Handle push bars

Wheel

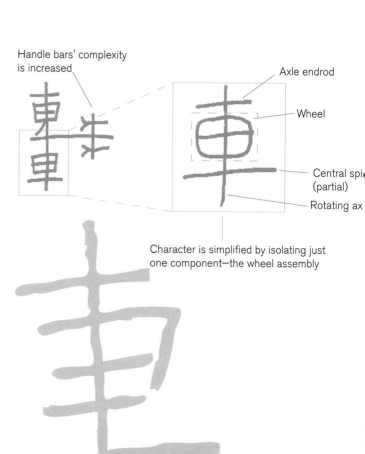

Handle bars' complexity
is increased

Axle endrod

Wheel

Central spi
(partial)

Rotating ax

Character is simplified by isolating just
one component—the wheel assembly

The origin of the Chinese written language can be traced back six thousand years, to pictorial symbols engraved by knives into turtle shells and animal bones. Known as *jiaguwen,* or "Oracle Bone Inscription," its "written" form adhered closely to the object it represented. The shape and volume of the object were retained in outline, while certain details, such as the limbs of an animal or the shape of a human body, still featured prominently. Most importantly, each element of the word was customized to faithfully represent its corollary in the object. The wings of a bird, for example, were drawn from nature, without any interpretative subjection to a written system. The earliest period of this form of writing lacked both standardization and a procedure for assembling words from constituent parts. The resulting etymology relied more on referential recognizability than on an abstraction that distilled the essence of the object into communicative components.

"Wheel" component is standardized by replacing curved lines with straight strokes

Shape and form of wheel are lost through simplification. Replaced by diagonal and horizontal strokes that merely occupy the space of the previous version

Comparatively, the luxury mixed-use project Pangu Plaza, situated adjacent to the Bird's Nest within the 2008 Olympic complex, deploys a curved facade and elongated building site to evoke the image of a dragon. Like *jiaguwen,* the building literally copies the shape of a dragon's head within its form; Taiwanese architect C.Y. Lee's abstraction or reinterpretation of this reference remains minimal. Lee's Plaza lacks design sophistication because it relies on shaping the exterior curves of the facade in an exaggerated fashion in order to enact its legibility. Just as *hanzi* are considered undeveloped when they have strokes and lines that follow the contours of the object they represent, a fully refined metaphorical design should not sacrifice elegant architectural form for the sake of pictorial veracity.

The next major evolutionary phase in *hanzi* was the "Small Seal Script," or *xiaozhuan.* It was developed to solidify the new unity of the country; the Qin Empire encouraged the standardization of the written language into a simpler and more systemized form. Even though the writing did bear similarities to the more primitive *jiaguwen,* where distinct parts of the represented object were still identifiable, *xiaozhuan* moved a step away from drawing pictures and toward abstract symbols that were more suitable for writing. The general size of each individual character was standardized to fit into a small imaginary square. Fewer strokes were needed to form a word, and a nascent effort was made to regularize the different parts of the characters into a systemized catalogue. The characters became more symmetrical as irregularities from earlier forms were dropped, and the shape and form of the characters became more adapted to the writing instruments of the time, which had developed from knife etching to brush-and-ink calligraphy. In short, the *hanzi* could now be called a systemized form of writing.

Foster + Partners' interpretation of the dragon for Beijing's new Capital International Airport could be compared to the advancing degree of abstraction in *xiaozhuan.* Like

C. Y. Lee, Pangu Plaza, Beijing, China, 2008.

Foster + Partners, Beijing Capital
International Airport, Beijing,
China, 2008.

xiaozhuan, the design simplifies the irregularities of the object form and systematizes components in order to better integrate within the overall architectural context. Three main design strategies are used to convey the metaphor of a dragon. With a curvy outline and a rounded volume that bulges high in the center and gradually tapers off in the terminal wings, the form of the airport is an abstraction of a dragon lying on the tarmac. Even though distinct body parts such as limbs, a tail or a head are not articulated, the structure is suggestive enough to communicate the idea of an organic, animalistic form. The red roof references the traditional color of Chinese dragons and is an improved way to communicate through standard architectural decisions, but we should note that Foster + Partners stopped short of abstracting the color itself. In addition, the dragon's scales have been interpreted as triangular skylights which perform both architecturally and metaphorically. This kind of productive abstraction parallels *xiaozhuan's* standardized yet still allusive components for its characters.

The final evolution of written Chinese resulted in more sophisticated abstraction and interrelation. The "Square Script," or *kaishu,* was introduced a thousand years ago; the fact that it remains in use today is a testimony to its degree of usability and refinement. The Square Script reduced the remaining ideogramic idiosyncrasies by denoting concrete objects through a few simple abstract lines. Its square structure and smooth, level lines were easier for common people to master. Its increased accessibility also facilitated the development of a fully standardized catalogue of character components that could be mixed and matched to create different words. In *kaishu,* the original imitative qualities of the character are almost fully translated into the abstract code of a written system. This, however, is not to say that all pictorial roots have been lost: the modern *hanzi* still contains traces of its object-oriented roots embedded within its system, accessible to every literate Chinese person as both communicative sign and indexical, historical metaphor.

Similarly, the soaring Shanghai Tower, designed by Gensler, approaches an analogous hybridity of systemic clarity in combination with metaphoric meaning in architecture. Like the *hanzi* script, every aspect of its design plays a practical (architectural) role, while concurrently suggesting the metaphor of a dragon. The vertical tapering and twisting form of the tower is evocative of an image of an uncoiling dragon hurtling toward the sky, suggesting torque and movement without referencing a single specific anatomical element of a dragon. In the case of the Shanghai Tower, *the entire building is the metaphor*. There is no need to designate architectural components for specific metaphoric roles to which the rest of the building fails to contribute: metaphor and function are integrated. Like the Chinese script, where the double layer of meaning is only accessible to those with a deep knowledge of the language and the metaphoric culture of that country, the Shanghai Tower's specific interpretation as a dragon is dependent on the contingent interchange between the design, its context, and continual public interpretation and recognition.

By becoming accessible as both a programmed space and a meaningful symbol, metaphoric design within the context of Chinese culture offers a means for dialogical, dynamic and interactive architectural exchange. While it alludes to a shared body of cultural meaning and value, its appropriateness is contingent on the daily judgment and acceptance of each member of the public. This continually enacted call and response is why metaphoric architecture in China offers the possibility for an innovative kind of critical regionalism, applied on discrete terms. Presenting a way forward for Chinese architecture by recovering something from the past, it embraces an understanding of the value of cultural objects by employing broad strokes of allusion—a propensity which has always remained latently embedded in Chinese calligraphy, philosophy and imagination.

Gensler, Shanghai Tower, Shanghai,
China, 2014.

HOW TO INTERVENE

PART TWO

Brett Albert

Classic, Cool and Customizable

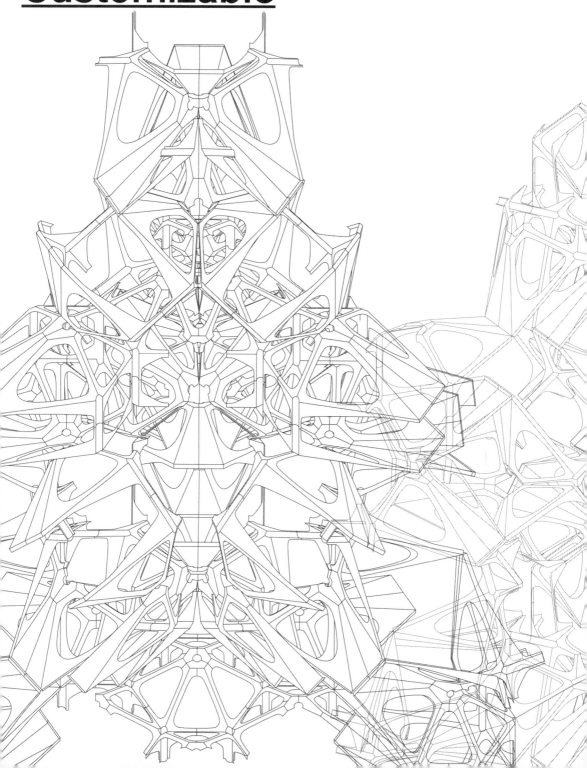

The Guthrie House, a project recently completed by the Chilean firm Assadi and Pulido, has been featured frequently and prominently in a variety of architecture magazines and design blogs. The architects were approached by a real estate company to design a mid-sized house with a clear and marketable identity that could be easily reproduced on a sloped hillside without costs exceeding the reach of the average, young Chilean family. In what has been framed by the architects themselves and others who have reviewed their work as a courageous move by a pair of intrepid young designers, Assadi and Pulido resisted what they deemed the inexcusably commercial and superficial implications of the assignment by designing a completely subterranean house. Burying the architecture not only totally eradicated its presence on the street, thereby removing any possibility for a recognizable image, but also created a requirement for an underground entry sequence that was entirely contingent on the particularities of the site. Faced with a promising opportunity to develop a prototype for an adaptable and affordable product that could be marketed as an alternative to the banal replications of traditional house forms built without the input of architects, the designers chose instead to create an expensive and entirely customized piece of architecture. Designed for no one besides the designers themselves, the Guthrie House was repurposed for what they characterized as their attempt to denounce "sell[ing] fashion."[1]

This practice perpetuates a model that naïvely positions architecture as resisting and deterring the commodification of art and culture with reactionary and ultimately futile acts of negation. Speculative architects had already all but exhausted this disciplinarily detrimental approach some time ago. More recently, in response to the growing perception that architecture was drowning in esoteric theoretical platitude, a slew of incoherent polemics about projective practice and professional engagement emerged within the amorphous paradigm of postcriticality.[2] The limits of these discourses are apparent in the mission statement

of one of the most conspicuous efforts to give them structure: the 2006 Projective Landscape conference held at the Delft School of Design, which convened under the auspices of finding "an architecture that is engaged with the reality of the society in which it is embedded, but focuses on its own discipline instead of looking for legitimatization of its practice in just societal criticism or in disciplines outside itself like sociology and philosophy."[3] Postcriticality might have succeeded in dismantling the self-destructive tendencies in avant-garde architecture at the end of the last century by criminalizing theoretical autonomy for stifling innovation and production. In reality, however, it has failed to produce any generative models for practice beyond reductive manipulations of tectonic and material phenomena.

The profession is at a critical point in which unprecedented opportunities for its expansion and optimization seem as immediate as its looming risk of becoming entirely obsolete. The accelerating dispersal of the profession's traditional responsibilities among an ever-growing field of specialists and consultants is exacerbated by architecture's persistent inability to achieve widespread recognition and appreciation by a general public. Architects need to both reorganize their practices to consolidate and optimize production, and develop tools and strategies for cultivating popular appeal in our increasingly media-saturated consumer society. It is impossible to accomplish this through cerebral references to obscure and convoluted philosophical texts or the manipulation of opaque formal indices. It is also impossible to disavow the social and political capacity of architecture in favor of formal novelty or vague and evasive

1— See, for instance, Nico Saieh, "Guthrie House/ Felipe Assadi & Francisca Pulido," ArchDaily, 13 May 2008, http://www.archdaily.com/773/guthrie-house-felipe-assadi-francisca-pulido (accessed on December 1, 2009).

2— See R. E. Somol and Sarah Whiting, "Notes around the Doppler Effect and Other Moods of Modernism," Perspecta 33 (2002): 72–77.

3— Delft University of Technology, The Projective Landscape Stylos Conference, 2006, http://www.projective-landscape.nl (accessed on August 7, 2008).

conversations about mood or atmosphere. Architecture has the capacity to negotiate between the dual and oscillating clichés of autonomy and engagement by simultaneously advancing complex social agendas, exploiting new technologies and engaging consumer desires through the strategic manipulation of image and brand identity. In order to do so, however, a clear assessment must be made of the current state of creative production and its relationship to audience or consumer participation. This assessment cannot neglect architecture's social responsibility out of fatigue in the face of ever-mounting complexity, nor can it stubbornly cling to formulas for social engagement that were crafted in the altogether different political, technological and economic eras of the past.

In addition to its importance in critical architectural discourse, the participation of the audience or user in the production of meaning was central to conceptual art, especially that of the 1960s and 1970s, which sought to dematerialize the art object itself into a set of viewer-participant relations in order to challenge and resist viewers' expectations and predispositions, and to provoke critical thought.[4] A sense of overt confrontation, however, seems less common in contemporary participatory art practices because of artists' increased tendency to address issues of consumption and (customer) service through the "design-art" phenomenon. In *Relational Aesthetics,* a collection of essays that attempts to reframe an agenda for participatory contemporary art through analyses of specific art practices in the 1990s, Nicolas Bourriaud dismisses many art critics for attempting to resuscitate and then take cover behind the intellectual pugilism of art discourse in the 1960s. During that period, a wide array of emergent forms of creative expression were discarded as depoliticized and complicit, superficial acts of consumer spectacle. Instead, Bourriaud advocates new models for producing or viewing art that are more appropriate for addressing the realities of the present. Rather than perpetuate a model that defines portable, self-contained,

individually received and often impenetrable works of art, Bourriaud promotes what he terms "relational aesthetics": practices which generate meaning through "the realm of human interactions and its social context, rather than the assertion of an independent and *private* symbolic space."[5] These practices form a framework for interactive and open-ended modes of reciprocity that are embedded in local, physical and social contingencies. He argues that these art approaches, while dramatically less utopian, are no less politicized than the art of the 1960s, even if explicit forms of resistance or friction are absent.

This "laboratory" model of social production encourages the transmission of authority in the production of space and meaning from the designer to the user, and the cultivation of formal and organizational indeterminacy. In architecture, an equivalent ambition often surfaces as a vaguely political project intended to subvert traditional oppressive hierarchies by challenging the notion that an architect imposes form upon the powerless either as an expression of his ego or on behalf of the will of authoritative governments or wealthy institutions. Individuals, instead, are given greater control and flexibility in the realization of their environments, not only to give them a sense of political empowerment, but also to cause them to be more aware of the social and ecological ramifications of their behavior.

From the articulation of sci-fi infrastructural armatures to studies of indeterminate component systems, historical architectural experiments with this motivation were too often reduced to a kind of method-idolatry, a pursuit of technological progress without social justifications for its necessity, or to projects that were ultimately dependent on technological and computational capabilities that did not yet exist. Today, the promise of

4— See Lucy Lippard, *Six Years: The Dematerialization of the Art Object from 1966 to 1972* (Berkeley: University of California Press, 1973).

5—Nicolas Bourriaud, *Relational Aesthetics,* trans. Simon Pleasance, Fronza Woods and Mathieu Copeland (Dijon: Les Presses du Réel, 2002), 14. (Italics original.)

ALBERT—

Assadi and Pulido, Guthrie House,
Santiago, Chile, 2007.

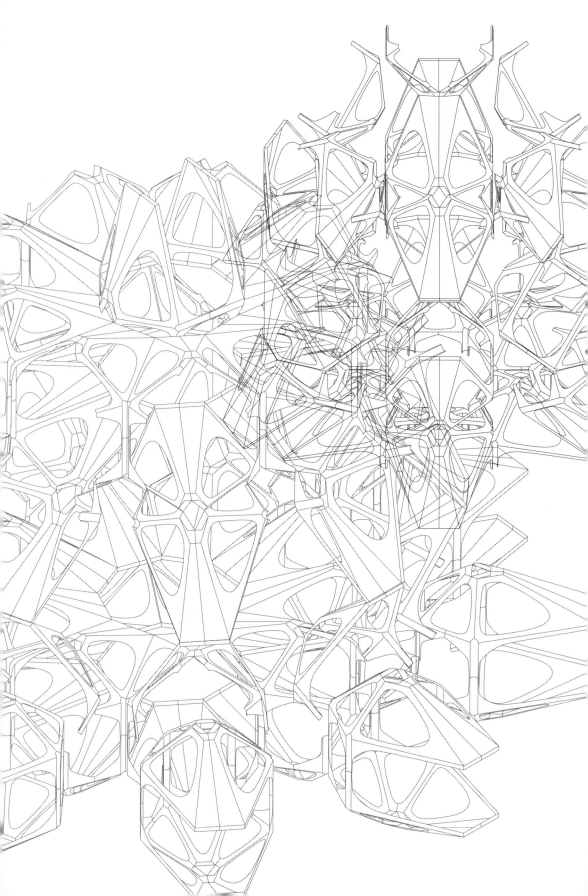

participatory design models has become a tangible reality. This is due to the advanced computational tools capable of building intelligent models that can incorporate feedback from their environments over time, together with new fabrication methods that make nonstandard, customizable building components economically feasible.

The contemporary paradigm of mass customization (that is, of utilizing developments in rapid prototyping and building information modeling) presents an alternative to the conception of architectural practice as producing static, one-off objects. Most of this work, however, is limited to a preoccupation with factory production that neglects any larger ambition to challenge the means by which users interact with and shape their environments. Stephan Kieran and James Timberlake's model for mass customization, for example, is the Dell computer: a framework based entirely on the manipulation of technical specifications without visual or aesthetic consequences. As a result, their approach primarily challenges production methods and delivery systems without generating any logic about how new technologies can change the way people who are not architects think about architecture.[6]

Other, more agile, design professions like industrial design have enjoyed greater success through their incorporation of participatory models. There seems to be a surplus of rhetoric in the architectural discipline about how to appropriate the success that industrial designers have experienced due to progressive technologies and streamlined, integrated assembly-line production methods that minimize the compartmentalization of tasks. However, technological efficiencies are not necessarily central priorities for architectural adaption in and of themselves. Architects have a tendency to fetishize the manufacturing processes and precision engineering of the automotive, aircraft and ship-building industries; these industries represent an illusive ideal of producing design products assembled with the newest materials and technologies, according to restraints dictated only by function and performance. While we should appreciate the efficiency and accuracy of these processes, we ought to focus first on the capacity of these disciplines to enable new social configurations through customization that are dependent on a compressed, operational time scale. This nimble and adaptive *pace* is what allows these processes to manufacture technologically progressive, recognizable and desirable products that serve as extensions of individual identity on a mass scale, while optimizing rather than disavowing their capacity to serve as generative social constructs.

One useful example of this in product design is NIKEiD, a website that allows consumers to customize their Nike footwear online, creating a simulation of the shoe in real time as users select its desired features. Although each shoe design can be tailored to reflect an individual's taste, the final product ultimately conforms to the Nike brand, whose ubiquitous presence in our society has become a social reference point. Brand identity is not a concept that is alien to architectural practice; in fact, one explanation for the contemporary surge of public interest in architecture is the trend for developers to use the names of so-called celebrity architects to market luxury developments, or the similar practice undertaken by large institutions to increase donor support for new public projects. This tendency, however, finds its parallel less with projects like NIKEiD and more with the work of high-end couture houses like Chado Ralph Rucci or Olivier Theyskens, whose astronomically expensive garments are status symbols for celebrities and the ultra-rich. While haute couture acts as a

6– Stephan Kieran
and James Timberlake,
*Refabricating Architecture:
How Manufacturing
Methodologies Are Poised
to Transform Building
Construction* (New York:
McGraw-Hill, 2004).

monument to the egos of both its owners and designers, NIKEiD's ambition is of a populist nature and contributes more broadly to the construction of identity in our consumer society. Some even argue that it was the rise of affordable global sportswear and casual-wear brands like Nike as effective cultural references that prompted the decline of many prominent fashion labels' couture departments, forcing them to channel more time and energy into less expensive ready-to-wear collections.[7] In an analogous manner, introducing an architecture that manifests a collective identity but has room for individual customization and inflection could help to upset the current domination of the field by a handful of inflated personalities who design extremely expensive and often wasteful structures.

There is, however, a risk in adopting the NIKEiD model directly in architectural production; the assumption that the presence of some form of consumer choice automatically equals political engagement is a potential distraction. To return to contemporary participatory art, critics have argued that art practices like relational aesthetics perpetuate a false and ultimately vapid model of implied democracy that devolves into a form of marketing. In her article "Antagonism and Relational Aesthetics," Claire Bishop warns that when "works-in-progress and artists-in-residence begin to dovetail with an 'experience economy,'" the theatrical deployment of "scripted and staged personal experiences" can be mistaken for authentic artistic production by and with an audience.[8] In *Design and Crime*, Hal Foster makes a similar point about the conflation of marketing and culture that omnipresent digital mediation has facilitated. He asserts that an object is no longer conceptualized as something to be produced and consumed individually, but is instead seen as "a datum to be manipulated ... to be designed and redesigned, consumed and reconsumed," conflating art and design beyond their reasonable limits and eradicating the "breathing room" that once separated culture from consumption.[9] Positive *and negative* forms of reciprocal feedback that

are necessary for the production of democratic relations have thus become displaced from participatory art practices today. When the possibility for negation is removed, a false sense of liberalism and importance is imbued in the plastic scenarios relational art procedures ask participants to enact.

A prototype for implementing a deeper level of user engagement is Issey Miyake and Dai Fujiwara's well-known series of A-POC experiments. These use a computer-programmed industrial weaving machine to produce tubes of material embedded with clothing patterns that form garments when a user cuts them loose. The pieces that emerge are not only customizable in fit or length, but can also repeatedly be transformed into other forms of clothing at the will of the user. A-POC utilizes digital fabrication and material research in dynamic, innovative ways in order to produce a recognizable, marketable and novel product. It makes consumers more aware of the ecological decisions they make in terms of the material used and reused as their pieces are cut from stock, transformed over time, and potentially recycled into new forms. Perhaps most importantly, however, A-POC so intimately engages users in the design of the final piece that their decisions affect both the product's aesthetic outcome—which in turn expresses the user's identity—and the product's performance in response to external and environmental stimuli.

Producing art and architecture is obviously more complicated than selling shoes. Buildings are complex manifestations of myriad economic, political and ecological forces. However, architects may still be able to

7— See Tim Jackson and David Shaw, *The Fashion Handbook* (New York: Routledge, 2006), 35.

8— Bishop, "Antagonism and Relational Aesthetics," 52.

9— Hal Foster, *Design and Crime and Other Diatribes* (New York: Verso, 2002), 21.

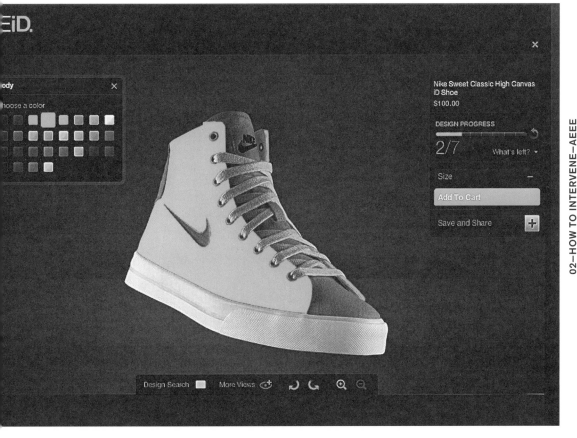

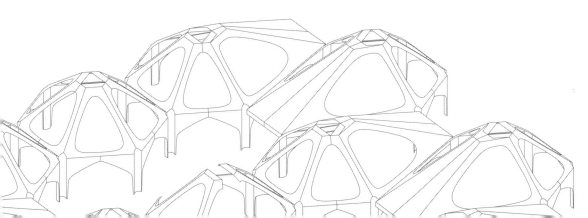

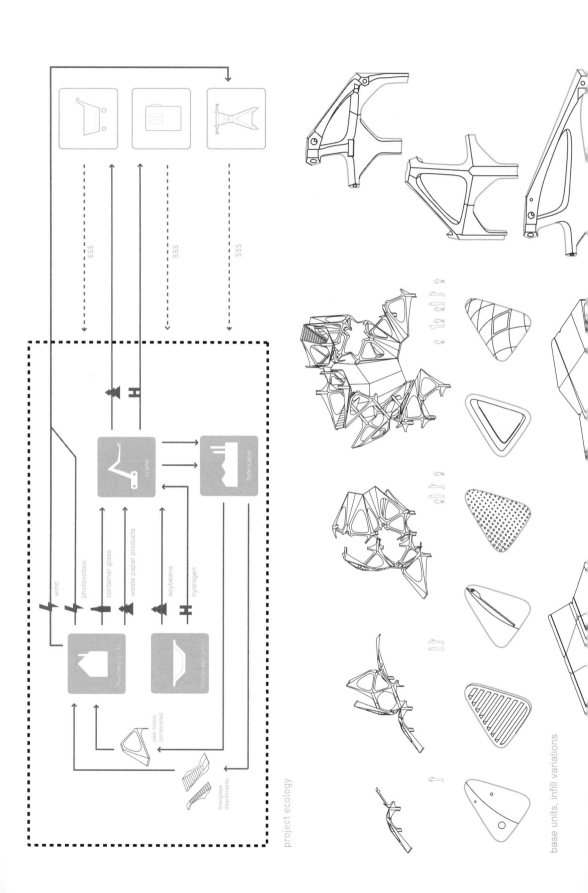

project ecology

wind
photovoltaic
container glass
waste paper products
soybeans
hydrogen

crane

fabricator

housing units

landscape units

cast biosip composites

fiberglass attachments

$$$

$$$

$$$

base units, infill variations

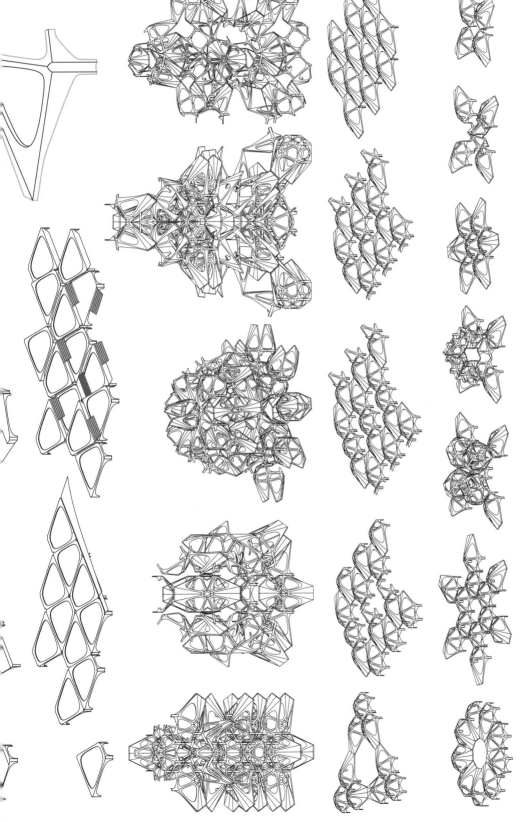

benefit from reimagining architecture, especially housing, as the production of customizable multiples. By extending customization to engage the user in a meaningful way while resisting the notion that all aspects, systems or components of building construction should be user-determined, architects could present a politically active framework within which more participants would be able to engage with environmental-modification processes.

The successes of the fashion and product-design worlds should be studied and celebrated as means for architecture to break free from its tired insistence on remaining outside of popular concerns, discussions and desires. Can we imagine architectural systems with the capacity to exploit emergent possibilities, create novel geometries and manipulate innovative materials through newly realized efficiencies in digital fabrication? The myriad identities and experiences generated by a truly participatory architectural process could evoke political and ecological consciousness about the ways in which we construct and consume our built environments. The contemporary paradigm of mass customization thus offers a strategy in which architecture can embed its users within the processes of architectural creation, aggregation, articulation, destruction and reconstitution, enabling new agency at both the individual and collective scales.

Design Ops

A conversation between Teddy Cruz and Jonathan Tate

Jonathan Tate— Interest in an architectural social agenda has reemerged over the last decade. Unlike the universalized and dogmatic approach to housing prescribed by the modernist movement, this time around the focus is on specificity: unique goals generated by local needs. As a result, the issue of participation has received renewed interest as artists, architects and designers seek new tactics for engaging with and responding to widely divergent pressures, opportunities and situations. Furthermore, the way architects and their collaborators practice today is often seen as more important than the product of their efforts. Your work has been heralded by many as a successful strategy in this expanded field. However, almost all of your ideas are untested in built form—it seems their dissemination is as valuable as or more valuable than their immediate realization. What do you consider most important: building or activism?

Teddy Cruz— Well, there's renewed conflict across the architectural ideological spectrum: on the one hand we find those who continue to defend architecture as a self-referential project of apolitical formalism composed of hyperaesthetics for the sake of aesthetics, which continues to press the notion of the avant-garde as an autonomous discourse, "needing" a *critical distance* from institutions. On the other hand, we find those who need to step out of architecture's self-referentiality in order to engage the sociopolitical and economic domains that have remained peripheral to it, questioning our profession's powerlessness in the context of the world's most pressing current crises. This reemergence of activist architectural practices, I feel, is also a direct critique of our field's recent unconditional love affair with a system of economic excess that could legitimize architectural experimentation. Such activism within architecture's limited spectrum is searching for a project of *radical proximity* which encroaches on existing institutions in order to transform them from the inside out and produce new aesthetic categories that can problematize the relationship of the social, the political and the formal. In reference to Guy Debord's war games, McKenzie Wark referred to the strategist as an activist who doesn't own a particular field of knowledge, but rather is interested in assessing the value of the forces that are inscribed and distributed in any given territory.[1] For me, this is the attitude that is really relevant today. Without altering the exclusionary policies that have produced the

1— McKenzie Wark, "The Game of War: Debord as Strategist," *Cabinet* 29 (Spring 2008): 73.

current crises in the first place, our profession will continue to be subordinated to visionless and homogeneous environments defined by the bottom-line urbanism of developers' spreadsheets and the neo-conservative politics and economics of an ownership society. In essence, then, the autonomous role of the architect builder is not enough—it needs to be coupled with the role of the activist. I don't see one as more important than the other because both are necessary today.

JT— Yet in spite of all of the interest, agitprop and dialogue, the main body of architectural practice appears to be quite content to operate within a paradigm you've defined as obsolete. This raises a larger question: is the activism in which you engage aimed at getting people to recognize creative work outside the traditional client-patron model, or is it aimed at improving everyday circumstances through architecture regardless of whether there is an existing paradigm which can support this work? I believe there is a need for architects to address important issues over and above a desire to right a failed condition within the profession. We have to move on if the true goal is to benefit people and places in the most direct way possible using the talents we possess as architects. It seems you are interested in redefining architecture (both work and works) as content—containing value in and of itself—rather than product. I wonder if that change can be accomplished within the accepted circumference of architecture itself. At what point do you become something else—a politician, say—rather than an architect? Are you interested in realizing change through architecture, or are you interested in changing architecture? And can you do both?

TC— These questions seem to emerge only from academia, prompted by the fear of stepping out of one's own discipline. It really gets me annoyed. I keep hearing it: Teddy, are you an architect or a politician? First, I think we have misunderstood what the "political" means versus "being a politician." Zygmunt Bauman put it clearly: the "political" simply means the capacity to anticipate a course of action.[2] To be political in our field suggests a commitment to exposing the conditions of conflict inscribed in a particular territory and the institutional mechanisms that have perpetuated such conflicts. In essence, it means questioning the hegemony of any particular institutional power. For me, it has been

2— See Zygmunt Bauman, *Liquid Times: Living in an Age of Uncertainty* (Malden, MA: Polity Press, 2007).

essential to understand conflict as an operational tool
which can redefine my own procedures as an architect:
What produced the crisis in the first place? The very
conditions that continue to produce conflict between
top-down forces of urbanization and bottom-up social and
ecological networks, and between enclaves of megawealth
and sectors of scarcity and poverty, can become material
for design.

JT— Don't such polarities just lead us back to the same
predicament associated with the failed modernist movement: an indiscriminate reaction to heterogeneous inadequate conditions that ultimately created a new, even
worse, situation? Perhaps we'd be better off defining
these issues as a set of imperfect relationships rather
than as conflict. The way we negotiate these relationships becomes the basis of the work, whether that's
through building or activism, or both, as you insist.
Maybe this is advocating for a soft touch, but I believe
it's important to come to a situation neutral, allowing
your position to be based on judgments in situ. How would
you propose we move beyond conflicts and constructively
participate in a more nuanced engagement with the issues
of concern?

TC— I am also not interested in such easy polarizations.
I am not interested in finding the wrong only to produce
the right. In fact, it is disappointing to see how the
institutions of architecture perpetuate the reductive
separation between the formal and the informal, the large
and the small, the social and the aesthetic, suggesting
an inability to think politically in our profession. I
am interested instead in simply placing myself in the
midst of such conflicts, to be informed of what produced
them so that I can empower myself to think politically
and to search for the reorganization of certain socioeconomic relations. The reorganization of the political and
economic "ground" is the only way, I feel, to produce a
truly experimental architecture in our time.

As activists, we need to rediscover how to reorganize
the territory rather than simply decorating the mistakes of stupid planning. I think that the material
for architecture at this point might not be buildings,
but the institutions themselves. As architects, we can
also participate in designing political and economic
processes. One of the most beautiful projects of the
last hundred years, in a timely way, is Buckminster
Fuller's *Dymaxion Map* of the world, suggesting that a
foundational rethinking of globalization started with

an understanding of the conflict between geopolitical boundaries, natural resources and communities. The
project becomes one of reorganizing those vectors and
the socioeconomic relationships across them. This is the
reason I have been compelled to acknowledge the marginal
as a site of investigation for my practice. In our time,
the new paradigms will come not from sites of abundance,
but rather from sites of scarcity.

JT— Yes. We're all trying to branch out from the
traditional model of thinking about and practicing
architecture because, first of all, that model is not
very responsive to observed need, and second of all,
we doubt it is sustainable. But broadening the scope
of our involvement may also mean that we give up some
responsibilities—diluting our role, in effect—so that
we allow ourselves the freedom to be involved in situations where we are not normally found. I'm part of a team
that is investigating long-term planning for a Native
American tribe on endangered land in southern Louisiana.
My partners are ecologists. The issues we're addressing
are primarily ecological in scope: How is the wetland
environment changing? How long will it be before there
is no land left? Can we reverse the situation, and if
so, how? If not, what do we do? There was a dimension
to our reply that was improved because the team was
capable of considering spatial and design needs, but the
architect's was not the main contribution. This experience has proven to me the value of forming nontradi-
tional collaborations as a way of producing more attuned
responses. This hints at new or at least different models
that can emerge from interdisciplinary collaboration.

TC— Absolutely. In fact, we need to completely rethink
what we mean by "interdisciplinary collaboration." What
is its operative dimension? As architects we can make
designing specific, tactical collaborations across
fields and institutions part of our design agenda.
Engaging interdisciplinarity means not only sharing
our point of view but also, and essentially, exchang-
ing procedures. In the last several years we have been
infatuated with notions of self-organization, systems
thinking, and temporal and evolutionary dynamics that
are borrowed from fields such as ecology, biology and
nanotechnology. But what we continue to import into
architecture are only the formal attributes of such
systems and not their epistemological and operative
complexity. Their *way of operating* can be a more useful device for redefining the political and economic

frameworks that have subordinated architecture to a mere decorative envelope. One interesting way of articulating this is the notion of deep ecology, as articulated by Fritjof Capra, which challenges notions of traditional ecological thinking at this moment.[3] For him, the deep ecology of a bicycle pertains not only to the functional relationship among the bicycle parts, but also to the understanding of where that bicycle was made, by whom, and its cultural application in situ. The political and cultural economy of a bicycle is different in California versus the Netherlands or China.

3— See, for instance, Fritjof Capra, *The Web of Life: A New Scientific Understanding of Living Systems* (New York: Anchor, 1997).

JT— In order for this way of working to be reasonable today, we've got to be comfortable saying that we face such radically redefined conditions that the entire equation involving the built environment has changed; that positive strategic positions are again possible if they don't already exist. If we agree to that, we're allowed the opportunity to think in sweeping terms once again, without succumbing to old deficiencies. Still, by expanding the role of the architect to include every-thing, aren't we setting impossible goals that are unsustainable in terms of the architect's ability to address them? Do these new agencies mean more diffusion and incompletion?

TC— I am not afraid of that. To be impossibly compre-hensive is a risk worth taking. But that is a personal choice. It would bore me to death to work on architecture for architecture's sake. I want to search for new para-digms that close the gap between social responsibility and artistic experimentation. I also know this is nothing new. (That's an important point.) Often when I talk about some of the projects we're doing at the San Diego-Tijuana border, where we are looking at informal urbanism, emer-gency housing and favela-like environments, people see it as a rehash of the "architecture without architects" movement of the 1960s and 1970s. I've had to start think-ing about what's different now from what was happening then, not just in terms of the general social context, but also why some of us are returning to these same issues. How can our procedures build on the past without repeating the same failures?

JT— The strategy does need to be different. Architecture in the 1960s ignored the specificity of unique

situational needs together with preexisting local knowledge and habits. The project, along with its solution,
was predefined. Perhaps we should begin to shy away from
strategies altogether and start thinking in tactical
terms. This is what I mean by specificity. We have to act
within parameters that we don't define, taking advantage
of the particulars of that spatiotemporal situation. Our
responses and partnerships should align with the task at
hand, unfettered by our presumptions of position, which
means that, to some extent, we have to eschew the historical concerns I've been referencing and move forward with
an agenda that responds to needs and not past precedents.

> TC— Well, it's important to understand that the past
> is not composed of isolated moments. There is a con-
> tinuum across those ideas and, in a way, many of us are
> rehashing those earlier attempts and their interconnec-
> tion in order to make sense of all this mess today. But
> let's not only recuperate the formal carcass of those
> movements, but also transfer and advance their ways of
> operating. This is when individual and collective prac-
> tices become complex and paradoxical. I think one impor-
> tant difference between today and the 1960s and 1970s
> is exactly that the work back then was being produced
> against a backdrop of urgency. There was a sort of col-
> lective ethics—a shared struggle—to defend the civil
> rights of the individual. Today the mood seems com-
> pletely the opposite. The backdrop is one of selfish-
> ness; obsession with individual rights has somehow been
> corrupted to mean only economic expansion and privatiza-
> tion. The sense of the collective and social responsi-
> bility have eroded completely.

JT— I have to disagree with the last point. Perhaps this
reflects a generational shift, but I do feel my contemporaries are concerned with these issues. The economic
paralysis we're experiencing has certainly accelerated
this, but the trend toward a broader social ethos was
unmistakably there already. I don't have to go far to
provide examples within the architectural community:
consider the continued progress of student-driven programs like the Rural Studio and independently initiated
organizations like Architecture for Humanity, which are
both offering new ways for designers to participate.
Additionally, no place is more relevant in our country
today than New Orleans, the city where I've chosen to
practice and teach. I am far from alone in this dedica-
tion. However, I would agree that we've moved past being
driven by a sense of collective urgency. Our motives do

tend to be more individualistic, but I believe that's an
improvement over indiscriminately advancing a collective
agenda. This brings up an issue I've touched on before:
if there is no widespread paradigm shift, how do you
expect the work that you do—pointed, specific and even
individualistic—to have an effect?

TC— You may disagree, but the headlines today are evidence that we, as artists, have lost the interface with
the public and that we are working in a completely different terrain. Just look at how this whole country
continues to be co-opted by the politics of fear, as the
"public option" for healthcare was taken away from us
so easily. The public at large remains hijacked by dema-
gogy that turns every socially based effort into a communist coup. While I agree that many students and a few
colleagues are reengaging with the sociopolitical, our
profession has lost its capacity to engage the collective
imagination. Even the most interesting of socially con-
scious projects, such as Habitat for Humanity, perpetuate
the idea that emergency relief efforts are about fixing
short-term problems rather than constructing communities.
Ultimately, it does not matter whether development is
wrapped by the latest morphogenetic skin, neo-classical
motif, some sort of bricolaged surface or LEED-certified
photovoltaic panels, if all approaches continue to camouflage the most pressing problems of urbanization today.

In our work, quite often the most effective kind of
project can be a minimal gesture with maximum effect. A
micro-intervention that can improve a specific condition can be really potent, especially if it creates the
possibility for other similar gestures. The difference
is one of scale (individual grand schemes) versus scope
(huge numbers of very small acts). The task of architecture today is to create a series of minor modifications
instead of a humanist utopia built on a tabula rasa,
pixelating the large with the small. Nicholas Bourriaud
urges creative practices to start *learning to inhabit
the world in a better way* instead of trying to construct
it based on a preconceived idea of historical evolution."[4] I think he sums it up very
well: the role of creative production is no longer to present the
possibility of unattainable alter-
ity, but rather to create new ways
of living and acting in everyday
spaces and situations. This implies
that we can contribute not only with

4— Nicolas Bourriaud,
Relational Aesthetics,
trans. Simon
Pleasance, Fronza
Woods and Mathieu
Copeland (Dijon:
Les Presses du Réel,
2002), 13. (Italics
original.)

"political architecture" but also with constructing the
political. Many of our small projects have begun with
urban pedagogy, social organization, and engagement with
political and legislative processes. That is what we aim
to do—whether by planting seeds of action within political and economic frameworks, producing tactical collaborations with neighborhood-based NGOs, performing the
actions ourselves, or helping to create situations where
creative micro-interventions become more common. I would
like to see more of our work built, but in the meantime,
disseminating exciting and hopefully inspiring ideas
through images is not insignificant. It's still part of a
valid and important process of fomenting change.

JT— I get the feeling that underlying your comments is
the notion of the master builder. In my view, that's a
position that tends to be problematic because it suggests that we should wear multiple hats or facilitate
many types of engagement independent of supportive disciplines. This limits the generative cross-pollination that
is arguably the most profitable outcome of our expanded
role, and it fosters the notion that architects are at
the top of the pyramid. This is an unfortunate, not to
mention antiquated, position that actually hinders our
ability to be effective in many of the processes we're
so apt to positively participate in and change. If there
were one thing our profession needed to come to terms
with, this would be it.

TC— There is nothing I wish to be farther from than the
idea of the master builder, which is such a macho position. This does not mean that I do not believe in the need
to take a leadership position. To be a good leader in our
time might be less about imposing a type of knowledge
and more about facilitating an intelligent conversation,
reorganizing the vectors of force at play in any situation, providing the tools for a new knowledge to be built
and enabling new models of possibility. It is a different
scale and gradation of control. Today there is the need
for a new type of leadership. I believe in benevolent
dictators, but not those in the shape of master builders
who use buildings only to solve the problem or manifest
their power. Instead, I am with those who first rethink
the relationship between public policy and collective
imagination. In this context, I believe that the role of
architects today, more than ever, is to facilitate new
and critical interfaces across fragmented domains, the
general public and institutions. We can be a sort of cultural pimp, facilitating new exchanges. I'm working with

the PARC Foundation, and part of the agenda is to think of templates where architects, community activists, NGOs working inside particular cities, and community-based organizations all collaborate on producing projects. The agenda becomes how to orchestrate and facilitate an interface between design, social organization and the kind of economic logistics needed to help us rethink affordability. So when I talk about taking leadership, I do not mean perpetuating the control-obsession of architects; rather I mean learning to use our training to creatively rethink how all of these participants can interface.

5— See Bernard Tschumi, "Six Concepts," in *Architecture and Disjunction* (Cambridge: MIT Press, 1996), 259.

Architects should stop worrying about the conditions of design and should become the designers of new conditions.[5]

In the end, the issue becomes very clear. If our current crop of designers were doing to social, political, economic, and institutional operations what they are doing to material surface and form, it would be amazing. In a similar way, architects that are engaged in the social sometimes reduce the actual formal and material qualities of their work to a kind of banal vernacular because they wrongly polarize aesthetics versus social responsibility. We need an expanded definition of innovation in both directions. We cannot continue to shelter ourselves in these camps. We need to really reengage these multiple spheres and reevaluate our own modes of operation.

Suzanne Ernst

The "Post" in the Post-Communist City

If city streets look interesting, the city looks
interesting; if they look dull, the city looks dull.
—Jane Jacobs[1]

Budapest is a cityscape in perpetual transition. Roman
ruins lie among early Magyar defenses and the grand
Renaissance projects of Matthius Corvinus, massy
Ottoman bathhouses glower in the shadows of ornate
Habsburg facades, and the regular volumes of the
industrializing nineteenth century break at the city's
edges into the mundane and vast geometrical patterns
of Soviet housing blocks. Connecting all of these
variegated urban layers is the rhythm of street bollards
that everywhere defines the experience of this city.

1— "A city sidewalk by itself is nothing. It is an abstraction. It means
something only in conjunction with the
buildings and other uses that border
on it, or border other sidewalks very
near it.... Streets and their sidewalks,
the main public places of a city, are its
most vital organs. Think of a city and
what comes to mind? Its streets." Jane
Jacobs, *The Death and Life of Great
American Cities* (New York: Random
House, 1961), 29.

These "Demszky posts" are spaced roughly a meter apart, in row upon row throughout Budapest. They are named after the current mayor, the first and only mayor of post-communist Budapest, Gábor Demszky. Within Budapest's area of 525 square kilometers, there are over 30,500 posts concentrated mostly inside the city center. Marking the boundary between vehicular and pedestrian space, their overwhelming ubiquity goes almost unnoticed due to their monotonous character and regular spacing. The mayor's intention in installing these bollards was to prevent the intrusion of vehicular parking on sidewalks, but the Demszky posts themselves act as vertical intrusions in the pedestrian realm. They create a feeling of enclosure, if not encagement, confining pedestrian movement throughout the city. The paternalistic quality of these street furnishings recalls the desire for the homogenization and segregation of spatial and interpersonal networks during the Soviet era of urban planning and design.

Following World War II, "the [Soviet] city was imagined as a highly controlled organizational structure that provided little space for unsanctioned memories and pasts.... It disregard[ed] ordinary people's relationship[s] with place."[2] Recalling the memory of the city's communist past, populated with secret agents and the enforced guardianship of the state, the posts silently guard and govern the actions of the pedestrian. In response to this situation, the following intervention proposals draw from the tactics of stimulation, security and identity. The existing posts are retained while the ground plane is altered in an attempt to reinvigorate and reinfuse existing public space with somatic potential, drawing attention to and diminishing the obtrusive nature of the posts at the same time. The posts are given new meaning and importance through dual strategies of concealment and exposure.

2— Olga Sezneva, "The Role of Monumental Sculpture in the Construction of Socialist Space in Stalinist Hungary," in *Socialist Spaces: Sites of Everyday Life in the Eastern Bloc*, eds. David Crowley and Susan E. Reid (New York: Berg Publishers, 2002), 49.

Camouflage—Invisibility

Camouflage is a way to minimize overwhelming presences. During World War I, Razzle Dazzle was used to break up the mass of ships against the flat surface of the ocean. Deploying this complex patterning on the ground plane of the city rather than on the posts themselves makes the continuous pedestrian surface the defining and yet destabilizing element of the urban environment. Concentric circles and irregular patterning drawn on the paving surfaces help to break up the verticality of the posts. Color allows pedestrians to repurpose the Demszky posts' paternalistic function within the city. Rather than impeding, the bollards can become referential aids for orientation and navigation through the pulsing patterns of the painted city streets.

Definition—Creating Space and Stimulation

Public squares and plazas in Budapest are surrounded—their edges are defined by endless rows of posts. The spaces within these squares are often spiritless and bland, and as a result they suffer from neglect and vandalism. By dressing the ground plane using floral patterning reminiscent of embroidery, an important craft and tradition throughout Hungary's long history, the square is redefined and given a sense of importance as it is delineated from the sidewalk edge. The reflective silver posts meld into the landscape, becoming vertical points within the floral patterning, ever present but invisible.

Safety—Security

Although the posts are supposed to function as security measures for pedestrians, their ubiquity has rendered them dangerous in their own right. Pedestrians frequently walk into bollards which have been placed in the center of pedestrian paths to mark off intersections with vehicular access points. Accentuating only the posts most critical to safety, at cross-walks and other places where people and automobile traffic tend to intersect, allows pedestrians to distinguish and pay attention to these nodes. Both the ground plane and the defining posts in these zones could also be colored to provide a clear delineation between pedestrian and vehicular space and the points at which they meet.

02—HOW TO INTERVENE—AEEE

ERNST—2

Hair Shirts —

A conversation between Sanford Kwinter and Marrikka Trotter

Marrikka Trotter— After the prolonged cri d'amour about
the ability for novel architectural forms, sensory
experiences and optic and haptic effects to open up new
apertures for experiencing and imagining the world,
many critics and theorists have reached a more ambiguous consensus. Newness—as staggering beauty or ugliness,
shock, sensorial flooding, amoeboid forms, folded planes,
et cetera—is being metabolized by existing systems of
power, especially capitalist systems of consumption,
at a faster rate than perhaps ever before. Do you think
that aesthetic or formal innovation can ever serve purposes other than temporarily taunting the status quo? Or
will architecture have to redefine the location of its
cultural value if it wants to resist this digestion?

Sanford Kwinter— If capitalism today appears to be enjoy-
ing an amnesty from challenge by contemporary society
and thought, it has certainly not settled into any fixed
or stable form for that. Capitalism is both diverse and
eternally labile in its forms. There is today not one
capitalism but myriad ones, and even these—Russian,
Chinese, Scandinavian, Anglo Saxon, Singaporean, and
so on—continue to transform, mutate and adapt to religious, economic, regional and ideological influences and
developments. When a medium is this dynamic, opportunities for new arrangements and interactions present themselves endlessly; you can count on this as surely as you
can count on death and taxes. No one can know if the age
of contestatory ideologies is over, but it would be wise
today to act and think as if it were. Such a posture does
not by any means call for resignation—rather, the contrary—it calls simply for openness, inventiveness and
flexibility. We must not lose sight of the certain fact
that the current social and economic dispositions will
change (indeed, this very week, both the *New York Times*
and CNN have reported that had the American Treasury not
intervened to buy out the insurer AIG, the entire global
financial system would have collapsed). The question is
always: "what social and intellectual resources will we
have prepared for ourselves in the earlier halcyon days
for use or deployment today?"

In times of crisis, rapid change or great adaptive pressure, forces are released—wild ones, experimental ones—that seek (require) new pathways of discharge, new alliances and combinations, even in a blind and random way. These are the moments when unforeseeable things happen, when bona fide change occurs and when history makes itself. Long views are worryingly rare these days, and difficult to sustain, but cultivating a "historical sense" is a way to continually remember that we got where we are by transformation, and by transformation we will be carried further on. This is where aesthetic and formal innovation becomes important. To invest in what may yet arrive, or simply in what is not here, is to project into history—into the future—a letter of sorts, or an engine, free to combine with forces that strictly speaking are not yet here but are to come. I hold it to be a sterile fallacy that we are mandated to design for the world and the conditions in which we currently live. Design cannot pretend to address the future scientifically (except insofar as that future is but a quantitative unfolding of present conditions), so it must simply set about to invent what is not yet here and—preeminently—to resist the logic of what is.

The ironic thing about contemporary capitalism is that it too loves and lives by innovation (especially pseudo-innovation, but it is largely incapable of and unconcerned with discerning between false and real). So far as I can see there is no significant cost to producing resistant, revolutionary or provocative and untimely work today. Many brilliant words have been written about capitalism and its inherent antagonism to "history"; but history, like time, is something you cannot cheat. It will return, powerfully and ineluctably, to gather, redistribute, and take back what it earlier gave out. These moments will always favor the untimely, the irreducible, the resistant and the new—that is, those things which were never fully combusted and absorbed into the previous regime or status quo. There is an almost magical phenomenon known to physicists as "poisedness" and to mathematicians as "hysteresis"; these related terms describe states of a system in which they are "pregnant" with imminent change. The processes and forces that result in new forms are already unleashed, but the

work of reforming is still taking place and not yet visible. Even for water to reach a boil, it must hover at
100 degrees centigrade for quite some time to gather the
extra energy required by its specific heat capacity to
carry it across the singularity into the gas state. Even
if we don't necessarily know the location or timing of
history's singularities, we know the direction. It is
the job of design simply to move that way (preferably
with some joy)... and wait.

MT– Unless... we are so eager to connect formal architectural novelty to cultural, scientific or technological
developments elsewhere that we misconstrue weight gain
as pregnancy. I find the application of a "discovery narrative," proceeding via paradigm shifts, to a discipline
that never seems to require a corresponding redefinition
of its broad terms of criticism somewhat disingenuous.
If this economic crisis turns out to genuinely *require* a
deeper level of adaption, it seems possible that architecture will discover that it is so out of shape that it
is incapable of such exertion. On the other hand, architecture, like capitalism, is not monolithic, so whatever
fate awaits the indolent profession as a whole (as it has
been somewhat unfortunately delimited since the 1960s),
we still have the individual actions and decisions of
architects, designers and theorists willing to experiment differently.

I would like to see design discourse reassess two conventions. The first is the location of architectural *value*
within its formal effects: when a work of architecture
is heralded as, say, biological because it looks like a
bug or a snake or because it makes your skin crawl like
a bug or a snake. This seems quaint today when art practices and discourses, which have long been the definitive
models for aesthetic value, have begun to situate innovation within the socioeconomic, relational and ecological
contexts which were once seen as the purview of architecture. If even art practice has expanded to engage such
territories, how can architecture continue to survive
in the single dimension of the aesthetic? The second,
related convention is the appropriation of architectural
meaning from surrounding disciplines, and the corresponding reduction of architecture to the symbolic mimesis of
discoveries from other fields. In combination, these two

developments create a situation in which architecture
is first stripped of its own agency and then set to
perform charades depicting heroics outside its disciplinary boundaries. How else can we explain how Deleuzian
folding, a rich concept full of implications for architectural (and other) activity, became literal folded
planes in architecture—a massive deflection of deeply
structural critique to the *form* of buildings?

If it makes no sense to borrow conventions for architecture from an outdated idea of art, it is also hardly
admirable to paste achievements from other discourses
on this flattened surface and call the results progress.
Like many people my age, I suspect, I would like to
figure out how to *address* ideas, issues and discoveries
from surrounding fields with the full media and agency
of architectural practice itself, so that architects are
talking about how to join with or fight against various forces and currents with an arsenal of architectural
techne rather than simply *registering* these vectors in
passive form.

SK— I suppose the part that I am in disagreement with is
how you present the principle of agency. While it is not
uncommon to think of history as something that responds
directly to acts of intention, and to expect there could
be answers to questions like "what should we do?" there
is actually little evidence to support such a view. It
is a bit like natural evolution: you can't say when a
new species arises from the viewpoint of the moment when
it happens; you can only know, or say so in retrospect,
after all the similar and closely related organismal
lines perish and fall away, leaving one isolated and
distinct one standing. It doesn't mean there wasn't a
"revolution" at some point; there often has been exactly
that—the rise of eukaryotic cells, the Cambrian explo-
sion, the emergence of the human, et cetera—you just
can't locate it within a one-dimensional causal system.
I'm aware that many "humanists" decry this new way of
understanding historical process, but it is a nuanced and
reliable model of novelty. The traditional models do not
have much explanatory success.

It seems to me that the longing for an answer to the
agency question harbors a desire for certainty and

conformity. Conformity is always the enemy of creativity, and left-wing ("progressive") conformity has by no means been a benign force in history. Obviously one needs to cultivate principled actions, and it is critical to develop a clear and communicable theory of justice. But these are not specifically architectural problems (except when such issues are ignored within the culture of the discipline or its institutions). Architecture's simple obligation is to resist the platitude of form, and this means to resist servitude. The questions you ask are not political ones so much as psychoanalytic and social ones: the answer is how to invest the labor of proposing forms for others with a spontaneity that frees itself from conformity and servitude. This would already be a step toward a kind of justice. I don't believe in the mindset of the specialized "arsenal" (the entire world is an arsenal!).

Indeed, another profound thing we can learn from radical evolutionary theory is that the function precedes the form. In other words, the tool is made long before the form appears that it is its job to make. In sum, I see the political question—and the political struggle—today to be to escape, not to find, consensus. Architecture needs to do little more than exceed its traditional limits to become a radical force. Architecture is the discipline that thinks the relationship between society and form. It ties form to social routines and it frees them from it. The question, as you well point out, is to not confuse the one action with the other.

<u>MT</u>— To conflate agency and humanism as though being capable of acting is somehow intractably human-centric is actually to ignore that evolutionary history is one of individual *struggle*—against foes and with allies in the terrifying context of disinterested forces. I see no reason why humans as organisms and flows of organisms in the larger currents of history, life and change should passively forfeit any ability they have to manipulate the systems from which they are inextricable. Furthermore, I think the concept of evolution has been much abused in its application to architecture. The laissez-faire system which has cushioned and numbed "liberal" western thought is not a reflection of the

natural order but rather a vapid shrug-off of precisely
those natural responsibilities which remain regardless
of how we ignore them. All life struggles to survive, to
outwit its natural enemies, to devour its food, to mul-
tiply, to flourish and to expand its habitat—in short,
to change its circumstances. Understanding that human
life is not the only life but part of life in general,
the reasonable conclusion is that humans should struggle
too, and that we have a responsibility to our humanness
and to the rest of nature to struggle. Participation is
not optional.

And of all disciplines, surely a creative enterprise
like architecture, which operates on and with such overt
and powerful vectors, should foment holistic interweav-
ings of humans and human deeds with everything else in
the universe. Instead, the evolutionary model has been
used to perpetuate the dualistic fiction of man as a passive tourist among massive eddies of history. Because
the supposed scale (which is really scope) of such currents renders human action insignificant, if not imaginary, architectural engagement with the forces which
render one project in substance and keep another on paper
is seen as impotent.

Furthermore, the elevation of the aesthetic-formal to
a position of singular resistance or abrasiveness in
the rush of other vectors of power is deceptive unless
it is coupled with the realization that such a position is itself a human action. Aesthetic effects are
not a priori resistances but actually devices people
have appropriated in order to address their own situations. By reducing architecture to a fleeting sticki-
ness which we have authored and which we deny authoring,
we problematize not only this discipline but also all
creative enterprise. We mistakenly assume that we cannot effect change in the large at the same time that we
create powerful moments in our own imaginations in order
to sustain the comforting idea that the lifeworld around
us harbors "natural" (i.e. not of our doing) pockets of
resistance that are innately built into the fabric of
existence. In so doing, we deny our responsibility to
understand the power—indeed, the agency—we possess and
to use that power and agency to struggle for the habitat
we wish for.

Having said all that, I certainly don't see attempts
to engage directly with larger flows and forces *architecturally* as humanist solutions in a heroic sense—*the*
answers—but as necessary (and already underway) addi-
tions to formal innovation. This is not to imply that
form is not deeply meaningful, but to point out that
there is no reason that attributes that you relegate to
psychoanalytic and social realms cannot be architectural
as well. The point you raise about function and form
has a direct bearing on this issue. There is a "function" that already preceded and may have even neces-
sitated the alternative "forms" of practice we begin
to see tested out at the boundaries of the profession.
This "function" is the preexisting, habitual and inces-
sant appropriation of space by people who have no formal
power to possess it, from de Certeau's subversive pedestrians to the squatters in illegal slums all over the
world. Certainly the attempt is being made *in practice*
to fit an architectural "form" or tool to this shape,
whether by installing a funicular public transit system
in a favela (Urban Think Tank), mapping illegal property
use to rezone for community-funded micro-development
(Estudio Teddy Cruz) or designing a dressage area in a
community park to accommodate clandestine equine grazing
(MUF Architects). The question then becomes: does the
"function" merit a "form" in theory?

To me, architecture is both an action and an object that
acts. We know that architecture tends to be harnessed by
dominant power simply because it costs a great deal of
economic and political capital. The process of situating, authorizing and funding a piece of architecture can
often be unjust, if only in the sense that it often displaces other functions or systems which are valuable to
weaker constituencies. Once the piece of architecture is
built, it can reinforce the dominant power that desired
and sanctioned it while draining resources from others
at the same time. Not all of these possibilities are true
all the time, but some of them are true most of the time.
If, at any point along the trajectory from desire to
dust, there is an opportunity to prevent or reverse any
injustice, I feel that to take it would fall well within
the bounds of principled *architectural* action. For me,

architecture is a machine for the shaping of the environment long after it ceases to be a shaping of the environment by machine. It is an extension of human struggle
into the full partisan noise of the universe. If we can
recognize this in architectural activity and discourse,
by learning to think differently, practice differently
and assign value differently, we may yet recoup some useful disciplinary muscle.

SK— Well, I generally don't believe that wearing a "hair
shirt" constitutes a political position. I lose my
bearings quickly when political questions are invoked
detached from specific struggles and contexts. Is "architecture" dependent on buildings, buildings on concentrated capital, and is capital irredeemably reactionary?
This may be true, but to argue in this way is possibly to
condemn oneself to aphasia. The logical conclusion is to
undermine thought before it even gets going. Are expensive buildings immoral? I have heard it said, but it is
hard to pay heed to such platitudes. I don't have a very,
shall we say, sociologically sophisticated viewpoint
about architecture, nor do I want one.

To offer my own counter platitude: I think of Einstein's
famous dictum: "Things should be as simple as possible,
but no simpler." I don't see why the following assessment is not sufficient (although I do not subscribe to
it): architectural production operates quasi-randomly,
polyphonically and almost, but not quite, blindly (it,
of course, is limited and constrained by multiple cultural, historical and economic factors), as if it were
a nature throwing out experimental organisms (or muta-
tions) and waiting to see which demonstrated the greatest
fitness vis-à-vis the environment. But in architecture,
there would be two systems of ecological constraint:
one would be the social and economic order—what the real
world wanted and could bring to pass—and the other would
be what we call "the discourse"—the imaginative frameworks, the eros, the critical rigors and rich environment of conceptual images that are shaped by specialized
observers that we call our critics, theorists, peda-
gogues, bloggers, journalists, et cetera. They belong to
the "pruning process" as well, limiting what gets proposed and creating specific vacuums to which designers,
in turn, respond. Some are overtly political in nature;
others are so merely indirectly because they transmit the
"function" to those who produce the form. But to imply

that desire, especially collective desire, isn't from top to bottom "political" is to miss most of what is at stake in any situation.

I see production as a deeply entailed process; I believe not only that it is possible to produce forms at a distance through writing (and I remind you that I cannot be the only one who believes this, as I am often held partly to blame for certain work), but that it is a responsibility of the theorist to *not* remain aloof from the interactive process. I was formed in an era in which a certain kind of "pragmatism" dominated thought: the Anglo-French "linguistic turn" that saw "saying something" as "doing something"... social existence is illocutionary. Many of my colleagues have assumed a posture of (ultimately disdainful) distance vis-à-vis production, something I have never understood. I have often wondered if it is that they do not wish their ideas to be tested in turn.

<u>MT</u>— The point for me is not to bemoan the weird and myriad ways in which architecture influences and is influenced by imperfect systems and situations, but rather to recognize that every part of this relationship offers room for creative and critical innovation. The "social and economic order" and the "discourse" aren't related to each other in any static, "infrastructure" and "superstructure" way. They intertwine and interdepend in a symbiotic relationship, both of them speaking and acting within themselves and upon each other. So when I say that the kinds of practices I have mentioned here merit theoretical attention, it is because their "doing" *in this moment* is already announcing this, and therefore we stand to gain by proactively expanding discourse to accommodate them.

Moreover, this particular strain of architectural effort does not need to become in any way dominant or widespread, or even to last, in order to be important. It is already important as a minor thread that strays outside the overall pattern and offers a connection with other wayward and fantastically innovative threads from the past. The practices of architects as different as Christopher Alexander and Buckminster Fuller both attempted to link up with the social, technological and economic order in a deeply discursive way, and where theory did not acknowledge them, they made their own: "pattern language," "tensegrity," and so on.

It would be unfortunate if, at the same time that we
begin to accept their radical contributions to architecture, we ignore their contemporary echoes. Part
of the work of theorists, as you suggest, is to argue
for the importance of certain works. If we choose not
to take a particular kind of practice up now, we simply delay the construction of its history for a later
date. The issue is simply *how long* we decide to wait
to consider innovations outside of aesthetic experience worthy of discussion. I view theory as a creative
enterprise which can itself be designed. The practice
of architecture can also create specific vacuums for
theory, pushing the discourse along where it is no longer adequate or cutting it off where it is no longer
necessary. The problem I see is not in architectural
practice, as it sends out adventitious roots in all
directions, but rather in architectural theory, which
in saying nothing risks stasis.

SK— These are sad times for architectural theory, I'm
afraid, not because it is being diminished by the discipline or professional opinion—quite the contrary—but
because there are few theorists left, almost no young
ones on the horizon, little disciplinary preparation to
produce them and a notable paucity of fresh or explor-
atory ideas and perspectives being discussed in the
schools and journals. The current sterility is partly to
be explained by the last decade and a half of professionalization in the schools, which has encouraged entirely
formulaic and parochial approaches to history. The recent
expansion of our PhD programs is a curious phenomenon
because it has reinforced rather than corrected perennial
anti-intellectualist tendencies in the field. Ours is the
only humanities field in which deep and broad knowledge
of adjacent domains—music, art, philosophy, literature—
is not routinely presupposed and certainly not particularly valued or encouraged. Regrettably, we are producing
people with a lot of note cards, but not a lot of ideas,
intellectual cosmopolitanism or ambition (and these programs sometimes make a virtue of this).

Our most creative thinkers by far are our practitioners,
but their philosophical training is less sustained or
rigorous than what a doctoral training can supply. The
field is moving quickly and decisively toward an ever-
greater worldliness while the intellectuals we now
formally prepare are moving in the other direction,
presumably because these programs are oriented to secur-
ing academic jobs. I myself find great hope and solace in

the current tendency toward dissolving the hard barriers between the design disciplines—buildings, landscape, cities, objects, communications—in favor of a broad approach to design as a form of thinking, toward a profession of creative conjecture. Antonio Gramsci taught that there were wars of "maneuver" and wars of "position" but that in the end, these two wars had to be resolved into but one. I, of course, read Gramsci while a student of philosophy and literature, but my migration to design theory was largely driven by my belief that architecture was a privileged location for this unification to take place. More than ever, I still do.

Yu Morishita
Notes on Residual Space

1—

To account for what were once described as the seemingly ungraspable "urban and technological forces" of the built environment,[1] the practice of architecture developed several methods over the past twenty years for codifying the relationship between given numerical data sets and the processes of design. By accumulating contextual information in numerical formats, offices were able to create simulation formulas that responded to dynamic environments. One important proponent of this working method was MVRDV, whose demonstration of how a given "datascape" could be translated into architectural language began to appear with their publication, *Farmax*, in 1998.[2] Meanwhile, large corporate offices like SOM amassed the computational ability to convert measurable ecological factors (solar, wind, seismic forces) into strategies for buildable deliverables, thereby expanding the parameters of the design process. These and other numerically based approaches effected a change in the orientation of architecture, toward a densified resolution of informational pixels and away from the exploitation of data for the sole purpose of defending architectural form.

1— K. Michael Hays wrote in his 1982 introduction to Fredric Jameson's "Architecture and the Critique of Ideology" that "architecture still has the important social functions of articulating urban and technological forces that might otherwise remain ungraspable, and linking the most intimate, local experiences of a site to the ongoing development of capitalism itself." K. Michael Hays, ed.,

Architecture Theory Since 1968 (Cambridge: MIT Press, 2000), 440–441.

2— See Winy Maas, Jacob van Rijs, and Richard Koek, eds., *Farmax: Excursions on Density* (Rotterdam: 010, 1998).

This search for increased data resolution has a precedent in the Enlightenment's introduction of abstract communicative instruments for the purpose of organizational clarity. These abstractions were neither nature nor truth per se,[3] but were necessary communicative devices that were secondary to the primary realm of the perceived world. Today, the qualitative values of abstract information are not suspect in comparison with "original" subjects: this apparent dichotomy was culturally digested by the realization that "abstract" and "actual" inhabit the same real space. Instead, we face a problem of how dense the data is and how it is utilized. Nevertheless, the uneasy correlation between then and now persists in the continuing difficulty of coping with immeasurable parameters, or the incommensurable values present in spatial practices.

Because these instrumentalities are no longer seen as derivative but rather as referential or citational in relation to the actual environment, it is possible that immeasurable parameters reside separate from the measurable parts of the world and the correspondingly parametric construction of the built environment. If so, the obvious question would be whether we believe that immeasurable aspects of life and experience ought to be negotiated as part of spatial production or left as latent geographical residue. But this leads us back to the old dichotomies. Instead of resurrecting a dualistic theoretical worldview, it seems more practical to figure out a way of capturing such parameters in a language that can articulate their significance in relation to numerically quantifiable data in spatial terms.

With this in mind, I would like to propose a reading of both unquantifiable and quantifiable urban qualities together, through the use of connective geometry. Geometry is a method of spatial organization which can recognize both kinds of qualities, as well as a platform for relating them to each other. Immediately new questions present themselves. Can such inflections and atmospheres, which are now available to human experience only through the senses and collected memory, be resolved as part of a denser data resolution through relational formulas? Is it possible to develop procedures that enable us to reinforce and protect these factors without limiting the felt actuality of the world through the imposition of norms of certainty? More questions still: Can spatial feelings or atmospheres ever become folded into the discourse of geometries? How does one understand one's context as a geometrical assemblage in which tendencies can be measured without formal determinacy and oriented toward potential anticipation? What would be the unit of measure afforded to the reserve of embodied values? In other words, what are we to measure of the world?

3— "The existence of this common measure makes it possible to compare all things one with another, and to submit them to calculation in spite of their natural differences (which are therefore abstracted)." Marie Jean Antoine Nicolas de Caritat, Marquis de Condorcet, "A General View of the Science of Social Mathematics," in *Condorcet: Selected Writings*, ed. Keith Baker (Indianapolis: Bobbs-Merrill Company, 1976), 186.

2–

Residual space within the context of urbanism is constructed at the interstice where quantifiable considerations and immeasurable forces meet. The notion of residual space is related to the recent discourse on "scape," which is an attempt to construct a continuous thread of relationships between the scale of an organizational representation of space and the scale of individuated physical interactions.[4] Residual space exists at the margin of numerical figuration—the space itself might present to us an immeasurable or indeterminate value, yet its construction carries the criteria for an alternative dynamic of organization within itself. In this margin, there is a durational problem similar to the biological formation of a spandrel, where the predictable assessment of its value is suspended and a lack of apparent or immediate use value can be addressed only through adaptive speculation.[5] Residual space is populated with *excess*: a density of informational and experiential resolution which functions in parallel with quantifiable urban aspects.[6] Because this excess presents the possibility for enriched involvement with the built environment, it is worth investigating whether geometrical relationships can articulate and relate such potential to the numerical cartography that is already the purview of architecture.

4– Alan Berger, *Drosscape: Wasting Land in Urban America* (New York: Princeton Architectural Press, 2006), 33–36.

5– "[A] spandrel is any space necessarily and predictably shaped in a certain way, and not explicitly designed as such, but rather arising as an inevitable side consequence of another architectural decision." Stephen Jay Gould, "The Exaptive Excellence of Spandrels as a Term and Prototype," *Proceedings of the National Academy of Sciences of the United States of America* 94 (1997): 10750–10751.

6– The idea of "parallel geographies" is countering the construct of "alternative geographies," which are not only manifested physically but immanently as an ideological construction. This can be seen where "scape," referred to above, is not solely reactionary to tabula rasa urbanism or utopian projects in which ideologically constructed instrumental geometries overlaid or erased the existing geographies and spatial geometries.

3—

Kyoto is perceived and marketed in many ways as an "ancient capital." At the urban scale, this identity has resulted in the cautious accommodation of new structures within Kyoto, regardless of its vast development, and the removal of existing structures that demonstrate mannerisms that differ from the symbolic image of the old city. This formal tension is indicative of a larger and systemic issue concerning the historical legacy of the city and its culture, manifested through its interconnected and yet mutually oblivious cultural metabolisms: one quantifiable and quantified, the other known but architecturally unarticulated. Investigating these systems spatially allows the introduction of what I will term "geometries of the immeasurable": a potential way to communicate the uncertain dynamic and durational aspects of urban infrastructure while simultaneously acknowledging quantifiable data.

02—HOW TO INTERVENE—AEEE

MORISHITA—

4—

The presence of an aquifer beneath the city of Kyoto was announced in 1999. A geological survey revealed that a vast natural basin lay within layers of gravel sediment, reaching the depths of 0.8 km and containing 21.1 km³ of water.[7] Water was central to the historical and cultural development of Kyoto. In medieval times, ancient and shallow wells dug in the confines of planted shrines and other communal nodes supplied the city's drinking water, while a system of drainage canals carried the flows of waste through and out of the urban limits. Over time, the groundwater became polluted by the increase in population and its urban waste. In response, in 1908, the city dug a new canal from nearby Lake Biwa and repaired and extended the existing urban canals, expanding their purpose to incorporate a network of water distribution. The wells, contaminated and released from infrastructural service, shrunk back within the foliage of the shrines, while modernization came flooding in with the plentiful water from the lake. The canals provided abundant irrigation and potable water as well as power for electrical generation, which in turn enabled the installation of public transport. Municipal greenery was planted along the canals, bringing secular plant life to the city.

Industrial modernity did not eradicate the old, however. The canals not only brought faucets to the hydrous environment of Kyoto, but also enabled the modernization of the sanitation infrastructure. The new sewer system slowly restored the health of the groundwater; today, both the modern, chemically treated water of the city and the well water from the shrines are potable. Nevertheless, the water from the canals tastes different. The well water, drawn from deeper strata, has fostered the traditional cultural production of Kyoto. The taste of its tofu and confectionery, the quality of the colors in its textiles—the value of all these forms of cultural production is dependent on the *sectional* property of the city.

The assumed quality of the well water, associated with traditional or historical values, is in fact dependent on the networks of modernity. The faucets, which the industrial age brought to Kyoto, can now supply either city water from the canals or well water from the shrines, connecting two different geometries and value systems in a single, co-adaptive ecology. The numerous wells and canals that run through the city can thus be understood as dual metabolisms of urban inhabitation: one acknowledged and coded and quantifiable, the other intuited, remembered and experiential, but both intimately accessible.

Although it would be difficult to attempt to capture this interconnected hydraulic situation in numerical statistics alone, a *geometric* overlay can be used to *describe* it. Kyoto's green space—composed of religious gardens and canalside plantings—is located at the interstices and intersections of these two metabolisms, diagramming the way imprinted local values intermix with the organizational patterns of modernity. A geometric schema depicting this existing diagram would allow for units of architectural implementation to align with both quantifiable spatial rubrics and the cultural desires of community tradition. The co-locational opportunity for urban greenery and public space presents units of manipulation at the scale of nodal adjustment, enabling other opportunities for architectural urban design. Acknowledging these implementational nodes when drawing geometrical resolutions in the grid-plot thus allows potential operations in hitherto-invisible residual space to become public possibilities.

7— The amount of water that lies underneath Kyoto is comparable to that of Lake Biwa, the largest lake in Japan. See Harushige Kusumi, Tadashi Furumiya and Shinji Nishimaki, "Study on Actual Using Conditions of Groundwater Resources in Minamiyamashiro District at Kyoto Prefecture," *Journal of Groundwater Hydrology* 1, no. 37 (February 1995): 55–67.

5—

These observations on the (tenuous) ascription of geometric values bring further attention to the terminological ambiguity of elements within urban constructs. The term "canal" in Kyoto most often refers to the aquatic urban infrastructure established in the Middle Ages and expanded and modernized in 1908. However, to the west of Kyoto across the Katsura River,[8] different features with different purposes share the same nomenclature. These are ancient agricultural canals for rice farming, constructed during the importation of Korean irrigation engineering in the early sixth century, and they have attracted recent interest in the context of Japan's celebration of its "national metabolism" of agriculture and produce.[9] These canals are concerned with topographical alignments and the surface distribution of water. The corresponding urban fabric, however, is a nongridded network of clearings of annual green rice fields within late-development residential areas. Cross one river, exceed a previously drawn boundary, and the interstitial green of our Kyoto diagram becomes a nationalist metabolism. Canals intercepting the urban grid become the grid intercepting the urban, while the same components shift and perform different functions in a dense geometry of overlapping relationships.

8— This river locates the initial southwest edge of the capital boundary, conceived in 794.

9— "National metabolism" is my own term for the Japanese Ministry of Agriculture's drive to increase the national production and consumption of Japanese-grown produce. See Ministry of Agriculture, Forestry and Fisheries, "Ensuring the Future of Food," (Japan: Ministry of Agriculture, Forestry and Fisheries, n.d.), http://www.maff.go.jp/ (accessed March 1, 2009).

6—

A 1565 painting of Kyoto and its peripheral areas by Eitoku Kanō illustrates a curious figure-ground parity.[10] In the style of the Kanō school of Japanese *byōbu* painting, the image employs a traditional technique called *suyarigasumi* (the use of gold leaf to create a mist that dominates the picture plane), which depicts multiple spatiotemporal dimensions of Kyoto. The gold mist acts as a visual margin of spatial transportation that relies on the viewer's tacit understanding to bridge the distance and duration between the events and objects in the narrative. It floats above and beneath various strata, carefully masking the residual spaces which surround the represented artifacts. Only isolated moments of vegetation are exposed, as the green of agriculture is nowhere to be seen. The shape and flatness of the mist becomes an instrument of spatial abstraction; beneath it are hidden landscapes, rivers and parcels of land filled with the residues of urban life.

10— Eitoku Kanō, *Uesugi-Bon Rakuchu-Rakugai-Zu Byōbu*, 1565. Pair of six-panel folding screens; ink, pigment, and gold on gilded paper, 160.5 x 323.5 cm, Yonezawa City Uesugi Museum, Yamagata, Japan.

Eitoku Kanō, *Uesugi-Bon Rakuchu-Rakugai-Zu Byōbu*, 1565.

If we were to address this painting today, the dense resolution of information available with our precise instruments would quickly fill the whole of the painting. The ability to numerically compute environmental situations would rub away the golden mist to reveal the abstract figures of geographical data on an unknowable and opaque ground. But the mist in the painting is itself both a figure and a ground—it acts as a fabric of spatial and material and geometrical properties which allows residual space its own imprecise yet positive articulation. Once it is cleared, the distanced spaces and urban elements discussed in this paper, all affected by the hydraulic history of Kyoto, become cognitively aligned even though they signify and operate differently, in different metabolic cycles. A geometry of the immeasurable could restore architecture's ability to recognize residues in spatial practice by allowing what were previously ephemeralized as metaphysical values to once again take on a shape and a substance. These shaped margins, positioned again among the refined resolution of spatial data, could articulate the co-appearance of otherwise unmentioned values in our world.

HOW TO IMAGINE

PART THREE

Joe Ringenberg

The Activated Space: Eight Pattern Studies

Pattern as Form—

In Kant's phenomenology, the experience of the material world is forever mediated by perception. The noumenon can never be addressed, and objects are unknowable outside the human mind, where our only experience is of appearances, textures and sensations but never the thing-in-itself. Our perception of form is not an intimate experience with a geometric reality; we confront the image and, in the dimensions of our imagination and the power of our reason, arrive at a concept of depth and volume, continuity, contour and form. If image is all we have, the altered image constitutes an alternate reality. Camouflage is not cosmetic, it's transubstantiation. Camouflage has the power to quite literally deform the object: the pattern is not a printed tent canopied over an airstrip, the pattern is a few acres of forest to the enemy bomber flying overhead. If form is but a conjecture of perception, the separation of illusion and reality becomes a category mistake. Likewise, the production of mood and atmosphere is not different from the production of architectural space. Peruzzi's majestic perspectives on the walls of the Villa Farnesina double the size of the room in every meaningful way, apart from how much furniture you can fit in there. The image of architectural space cannot be separated from space itself. As far as phenomenology is concerned, the pattern of form is all the form you need.

<u>Pattern as Play</u>

For all its economy and efficiency, for all its gravity, the city can feel like a skyscraping costume party. Whether the facade expresses the fundamental basis of a building's philosophical foundation or just the trendy treatment of the season, the surface is never entirely innocent. The facade that takes itself too seriously (the stern face of a New Brutalist monolith, perhaps?) is the one most likely to be hiding polka-dots within its untreated concrete. When the plaster was cleaned from the facade of the 500-year-old Palazzo Farnese, the brickwork beneath revealed the whimsy of the laborers. Provided with bricks of two slightly different shades, the Renaissance bricklayers could not help but have a little fun, making faint crosses and diamond patterns in the brick walls of the palazzo. Whimsy is a uniquely human characteristic. Pattern liberates architecture from predictability, humanizes the sterile and precise, and makes way for a touch of irony alongside all the complexity and contradiction. A touch? Deceit! Optical illusions, cultural cross-references, and downright duplicitous scales wage an all-out war on sobriety in architecture. Pattern is play in a field too full of the cut-and-dry.

Pattern as Ideology

Or, if you prefer, ideology as pattern. A system that subsumes all externalities and interprets variation within the rules of its own repetition: a pattern. The totalizing effect of patterns, in diagrams and filing systems, layouts and lab results, has as its primary end the rationalization of perceived chaos. When the practice of the craftsman is broken down into the steps of a production process, the intricacies of creation are either reduced to equivalent items on a checklist or entirely omitted. By abstracting the individual as a data point on a boundless field of repetition and variation, the pattern sacrifices the meaningful experience of the particular for the illusion of omniscience. The diagram does not satisfy the desire to know; it merely represents what satisfaction of curiosity would look like, if by experience we had come to know intimately some corner of the world. The ideology of pattern provides an image of satisfied curiosity that takes the place of experience itself; it implies clarity and supplies distortion. The pattern system presumes totality, includes all externalities, and reinterprets dissent as just another sanctioned variation.

Pattern as Narrative

The marks, stains, and layers of a surface read like a history, a nuanced timeline that produces a character from an object. Pattern reveals a narrative; it is the index of time. The honey color of fresh cedar shingles that gives way to a weathered and sun-bleached silver separates the new from the old in a Nantucket neighborhood. High-water marks and burn patterns carry forth a history of natural disasters. Oxidization, pigmentation, erosion and decay are pattern projections that betray genealogies and describe the lives of materials and the buildings which are constructed from them. But every true story is mirrored in fiction; patterns are just as powerful fabricators. The rusticated facade, the tea-stained parchment paper and the carefully composed scatter of houses in a fresh subdivision all write a false narrative of patterns. Narrative is as much fantasy as it is chronology. Pattern, likewise, can reveal as easily as it can deceive.

Pattern as Identity

Patterns and fashion go hand in hand, from talk of tipping points and trends down to the basics of plaid and houndstooth. In one version of the fashionable world of patterns, Jackie O. in Marimekko and Canal Street Louis Vuitton mark two extremes, with family tartans and school spirit somewhere in the middle. These patterns operate as signifiers, the value of which is derived from their ability to express identity as part of an organization, social class or lineage. As these prints fall in and out of fashion, their pattern is the pattern of a trend, linking consumers to changing groups, as much as it is a pattern of branding, linking objects to producers or certain handbag collections. The sought-after fountainhead of trends, the golden fleece of the early-adopter, is the protopattern which cannot be faked, only imitated. To that end, Wim Delvoye's pigs aren't social commentary on a new line of Louis Vuitton footballs, they're idols. They are an updated golden calf, whose intrinsic pattern reflects the dreams and desires of its worshipers, the god in whose image they wish they were made. The LV monogram must be a divine sign. Where permanent tattoos trump silkscreen prints, the final transfiguration is scarification, when the indelible pattern appears from within. These patterns, like horrible burns and the patina of antique silver, link their implications to the innate characteristics of the material rising to the surface. They are the real deal, pure and infallible. You can trust in them.

Wim Delvoye, *Louise*, 2004.

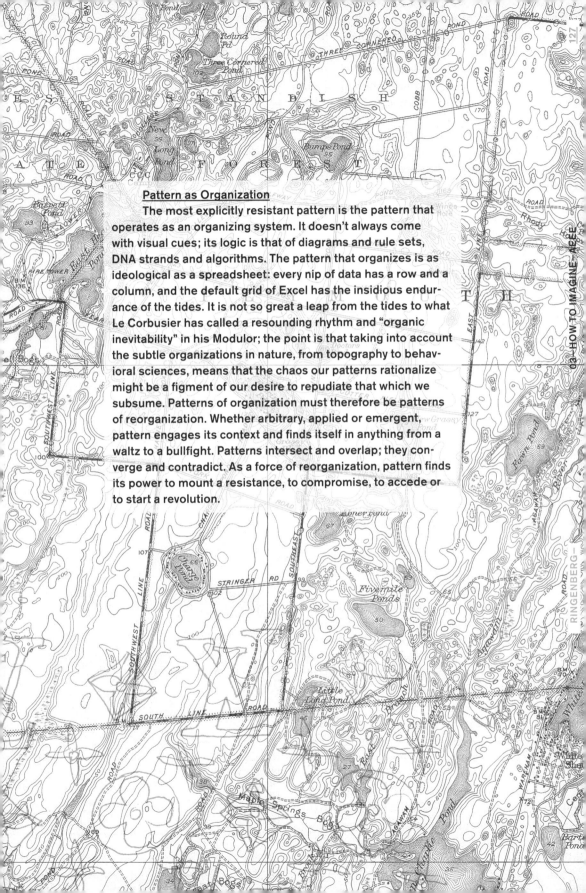

Pattern as Organization

The most explicitly resistant pattern is the pattern that operates as an organizing system. It doesn't always come with visual cues; its logic is that of diagrams and rule sets, DNA strands and algorithms. The pattern that organizes is as ideological as a spreadsheet: every nip of data has a row and a column, and the default grid of Excel has the insidious endurance of the tides. It is not so great a leap from the tides to what Le Corbusier has called a resounding rhythm and "organic inevitability" in his Modulor; the point is that taking into account the subtle organizations in nature, from topography to behavioral sciences, means that the chaos our patterns rationalize might be a figment of our desire to repudiate that which we subsume. Patterns of organization must therefore be patterns of reorganization. Whether arbitrary, applied or emergent, pattern engages its context and finds itself in anything from a waltz to a bullfight. Patterns intersect and overlap; they converge and contradict. As a force of reorganization, pattern finds its power to mount a resistance, to compromise, to accede or to start a revolution.

Pattern as Projective

…as the intersection between the inherent multiplicities of the visual environment. The meandering view encounters patterns of organization, in movements, on surfaces; and in the overlaps and engagements it discovers an elaborate performance. Sidewalk déjà vu, peculiar convergences and anachronisms arise in patterns, and by patterns are reconciled. The city street is a theatre of interacting fields where blurred borders project alternate histories hidden in layers of paint and fantastical narratives encoded in misshapen city blocks. Virtual realities arise when systems of organization meet and bleed into each other's territory. Pattern interferences and illusions that reveal themselves in movement and cross-reference describe a city of free association, where the allure of what-if draws the traveler beyond what-is.

Pattern as Index

An unpatterned surface is a blank screen. The projected pattern is legible in a way few texts can aspire to: it expresses the information of the whole on the whole. Fishnet stockings trace contour better than any topographical lines. Surface is read as the index of volume and, as such, takes precedence, just as the erotic image eclipses the model herself. Koolhaas's CCTV headquarters takes the discussion beyond volume and contour. The facade expresses the structure of the building—the diagrid pattern varies in density to reflect the distribution of forces and to provide the required reinforcement. The pattern acts as an index of the lateral and gravitational loads that the structure encounters, even as it fulfills the practical requirements of construction. The indexical pattern creates an object preoccupied with representation and self-reference; the index traces reality.

Re-enchanted Architecture—

A conversation between K. Michael Hays and Marrikka Trotter

K. Michael Hays— We should try to map out some of the characteristics of present-day thinking about architecture. Surely one of the things that is reconfirmed daily is an increasing lack of interest in architectural form, in the sense of the 1970s and 1980s *obsession* with formal issues and someone like Preston Scott Cohen's obsession with form. I see this increasing lack of interest in a simultaneous return to anthropological and ethnographic issues in scholarly fields like history and theory. Perhaps the awareness of the globalization of society and culture brings with it a suspicion of single buildings as objects that can be read art historically, and also a suspicion of form, generally. An increasing interest in globalization comes hand in hand with a decreasing interest in form.

Marrikka Trotter— Well, I think there is some sense that you can no longer pit contingency and autonomy against each other: both are constructs that have become less useful by themselves. Because of this, we feel the need to define a boundary to the discourse in a way that still allows encroachments and infections in both directions.

KMH— Yes. I think connections in general are important. But we need to be clear that when we talk about autonomy, we are not talking about withdrawal into some private, esoteric language game. Autonomy never meant withdrawal, at least in someone like Adorno.

MT— And that's been misunderstood.

KMH— Yes. Aldo Rossi was largely responsible for introducing autonomy in architecture, and when he did, he was using it in Adorno's way. That to me is very clear. Rossi felt that in order for architecture to have social power and impact, it had to first be architecture. If it tried to have social impact by being social directly, in some way, it would always fail; its social role was to be architecture first and foremost. Another way of saying it is that, turning to its own techniques, its own conventions, its own history, its own logic, is architecture's social responsibility as architecture. And I think that was Adorno's interpretation, and that's the way we want to use it. But even that is now suspect. The original idea was that if architecture could resist the encroachment of consumer society, it would be through its autonomy. We simply don't think that's possible any longer —the resistance model can no longer go through.

MT— I would say it a little differently. We no longer have that particular hope or construction that posits that

architecture can resist through the mechanism of autonomy. But I don't think that the resistance model is dead.

KMH— OK.

MT— If anything, the idea that architecture can and ought
to resist has become more necessary now than ever.

KMH— Yes. I do think that I like the interaction between
contingency and autonomy if we keep that formulation. To
develop that would end up with something much more complex than either one or the other; we would require ourselves to emphasize connections. It would also mean that
form would still have a role, but probably form would
no longer be lodged in an individual object; instead it
would become something much more spread out, expansive,
changing and mutating. But it would still be form.

MT— We have to come to terms with the fact that architecture is a complex and synthetic discipline which is
inherently contingent and relational. We are (rightly)
losing our faith in an architecture which is only valued through form at the same time that we understand that
form is still a necessary component of architecture.

KMH— Right. But I think people go to the extreme when
they say form is not interesting, and only performance or
effect is interesting.

MT— The odd thing about that is that the way they are
defining performance, performativity, haptic effects
and so forth is still driven by art historical terms and
art historical values. They are simply taking one set of
artificial and myopic alibis for architectural value and
replacing them with another.

KMH— Correct. That dichotomy is a false one, but it has
been assumed. Might it not be the case that a lack of
interest in formal issues has come about because the
techniques of design today seemingly solve some of the
formal problems for us? Contemporary design technologies come with a certain ready range of form, so that the
discovery, manipulation and elaboration of form is almost
discouraged by the design technology itself.

MT— The way that I would characterize it—I agree with
you—is that all intelligent architectural practice is
continuously looking for locations of roughness, because
these are catalysts for creativity at the end of the day.
When something, like form, gets a bit too smooth, or as
Wittgenstein would say, so slippery that it becomes difficult to walk, architects have to look elsewhere for

that rough ground. Right now, it seems as if there are very few refuges in formal manipulation that afford any kind of traction.

> KMH— I think the inability to find traction is because the practice seems to have lost interest in both the past as a reference—which I think is not necessarily a bad idea— and in the future as a goal. We don't see the present as a future for a past and we don't see the present as what will become a past for some other future, so we've lost both the sense of projecting backward and the hope of projecting forward. Traction could also come from a kind of renewed utopian or future-oriented concern, which is presently lost by focusing so much on the immediate moment.

MT— I do think we find it increasingly difficult to imagine that the present will be a past for a future. People are very uncertain about the future. There's a blindness about the fact that "we cannot escape history," as Lincoln reminded us. But I'm not so worried about that because I feel that history will take care of itself—you can't avoid it and it comes back anyhow. Indeed, we seem to be passing so quickly from a moment of irresponsibility into a moment of profound guilt that it may already be upon us. If I look for opportunities for traction in terms of the future *I* aspire to, I look for agonistic opportunities within existing conflicts. It astonishes me that, with all this slippery maneuvering around form, performance and effect, architecture as a whole practice hasn't really engaged in the desperate and important struggles that are going on. It's as if architecture is so concerned about its own survival that it is unable to get involved. And this is in spite of, as you put it, a very depressing tendency to treat architecture as though it somehow belongs in another discipline and can be called and valued by other things. In spite of this, we are not engaging in these surrounding fields in an active and specifically architectural way.

> KMH— Is the lack of engagement a symptom of general disenchantment? Remember that Weber's original notion of disenchantment was in part a lament that an increasingly rationalized, standardized and mechanized modernity was leveling and stripping life of former enchantments. The German word is *Entzauberung*: literally, a deprivation of mystery, a deprivation of magic. If our world prior to modernity was full of spirits and presences that we couldn't explain and couldn't even know, but which nevertheless somehow controlled our lives, then disenchantment was partly an increasing awareness of how things actually

work, as well as an increasing leveling and "demagifica-tion" of our lives as a result. This comes with certain consequences. The point would never be to return to some magical, mysterious, enchanted life, but rather to learn to live with disenchantment. Or, you have to learn to live differently now that enchantment is no longer pos-sible. The question is whether that model needs to be updated in our own time. My own initial feeling is that we accept our disenchantment too readily and too easily and without resistance.

MT— I think we did accept it without resistance. But the time has now come (again) where we find ourselves impelled to act, and we need some enchantment to do it. Enchantment literally means "to sing into being": it has the same root as "incant." I think this is what creative practice does. I see no place in it for negat-ing or refusal.

KMH— Well, I think that I certainly remain a holdout for the possible power of the resistance model, but I also am increasingly interested in the more hybrid, synthetic insidious models that belong to the interaction of auton-omy and contingency. I refuse to say it's either a matter of resistance or acquiescence. For me, negation is not synonymous with resistance or with just naysaying, and it's certainly not synonymous with refusal. What I mean by negation, and what is meant by negative thinking in the Hegelian-Adornian sense, has more to do with under-standing that there are more things that can be presented to thought than can be positively and affirmatively said. The substantiation of certain latencies further projects other things that must themselves for the moment remain unconceptualized and unsubstantiated. I think negative thinking involves presenting something that you don't quite know how to conceptualize yet.

MT— You're making a distinction between negative think-ing in the proper Adornian way, which you support—which is presenting something which cannot be presented by presenting the hole that it would make in space, so to speak—and the kind of thing that has often been confused with negative thinking—something like what Eisenman said in his debate with Christopher Alexander: "The role of art or architecture might just be to remind people that everything is not all right."[1] The latter is point-ing out that something is bad or that the situation is not optimal, and the former is saying, "I can't show this to you yet, but here is the space around it."

1— Peter Eisenman and Christopher Alexander, "Discord Over Harmony in Architecture: The Eisenman/Alexander Debate," *GSD News* 11, no. 5 (May-June 1983): 16-17.

KMH— Yes. The Eisenman version is the older model of
resistance and refusal, which is connected to the kind
of autonomy we already talked about as being defunct.
"I don't like consumer society, I want to refuse it, so
I'll make buildings that are all white and make people
uncomfortable, because I refuse it and I negate it." But
there's another kind of negation, which is forward-look-
ing. That point about architecture and negative thinking
is a general misunderstanding and a problem with the word
"negative." In order to state something affirmatively,
and positively, you have to have a code in which it can
be stated. There are times, and I think we are in one of
those times, when we want to project forward—we want to
move forward—and this is also what I think we mean by
utopia. We want to project toward the future. We want
to make the present a past for some future, but we don't
have the code in which that can be affirmatively posited
yet. So we find ways, and this is the negative part, of
presenting the possibility of something that we don't yet
know how to represent positively. That's what I mean by
negative dialectics.

MT— In that case I agree, absolutely. I think what all
architecture does is create something that was only
latent before, whether that was an emotion, an idea or a
flow of some particular power. I believe that, regardless of the abdication—or engagement—of its protagonists,
architectural acts are always ideological, social and
political. Architecture always substantiates, in some way
and to some degree, something that was not expressed or
available before. This process of bringing to the surface
is perhaps the defining characteristic of architecture.
And in that case, I think we have to not only reassess
our resistance to the idea that disenchantment is our
condition on a larger cultural level, but also reassess
our potential misuse of architecture in the service of
what we attempt to do as human beings involved in other
flows and other forces. It's not true that we can only
resist things and forces through negating or exposing. We
can also generate counterforces and, as you mentioned,
utopian alternatives.

KMH— In the same way that architecture substantiates or
gives perceivable or perceptible substance to forces
that were only latent before, couldn't it also present the potential for further latencies on the other
side? So it reaches back into a kind of latency that we
cannot see until it's architecturalized, but it also
projects forward other possible latencies that will be

substantiated, or conceptualized, or presentable later.
It is not refusal but is rather proposing that we look
for something that we don't yet know how to represent.
Presenting something for which there is not yet a code or
a symbol or a conventional representation—that to me is
what we might want to call a reenchantment. No—you know
what—I would *exactly* call that a "singing into being."
Contemporary architecture *must* learn to do that. We've
got to learn to use that singing into being.

MT— The amazing thing to me is how well enchantment as
"singing into being" defines the fundamental thing that
architecture does. It always sings something into being.
And in that act of creation, whether it's something on
paper, whether it's something mental, whether it's something physical—a building (whether it is in the service
of something we might call complicit or in the service of
something we might call resistant)—or whether it's simply
the exposure out into the world of a new way of thinking
or of seeing or a new possibility for action, it always
does that. Somehow we have artificially boxed ourselves
into a corner and because we have done this to ourselves,
this very act of agency disproves that we are incapable
of affecting the real. We have made up this fiction that
the part of architecture that counts is the coded part
that can speak to us, forgetting that architecture is
also a process that is both autonomous and contingent at
the same time. And that there are many points along that
long process where we actually have a chance to project a
different future than the past that we latently realize.

KMH— This is where "singing into being" connects with the
latency-negative thinking model. "Singing into being"
is different from abstract architectural intellection
because "singing into being" would produce something that
is prior to intellection and to clear conceptualization;
it might lead us toward conceptualization later, but you
sing sometimes in a way before you think, or more than
you think.

MT— Yes, exactly. I know that some people get nervous when we start talking in these terms, because
you start running along that track that starts out
with magical thinking and ends up with "we make our
own reality."

KMH— See, I could do with a little magic in architecture.
Not in the sense of irresponsible pied pipers, but in
the sense of what we properly call the sublime, in the
sense that architecture presents something that is not at
the time already representable. I actually think those
two things go hand in hand. By bringing latencies into
substance with the strange, particular language of architecture, it also projects forward things that we won't
discover until later. If that can be called reenchantment, then I could do with a little reenchantment.

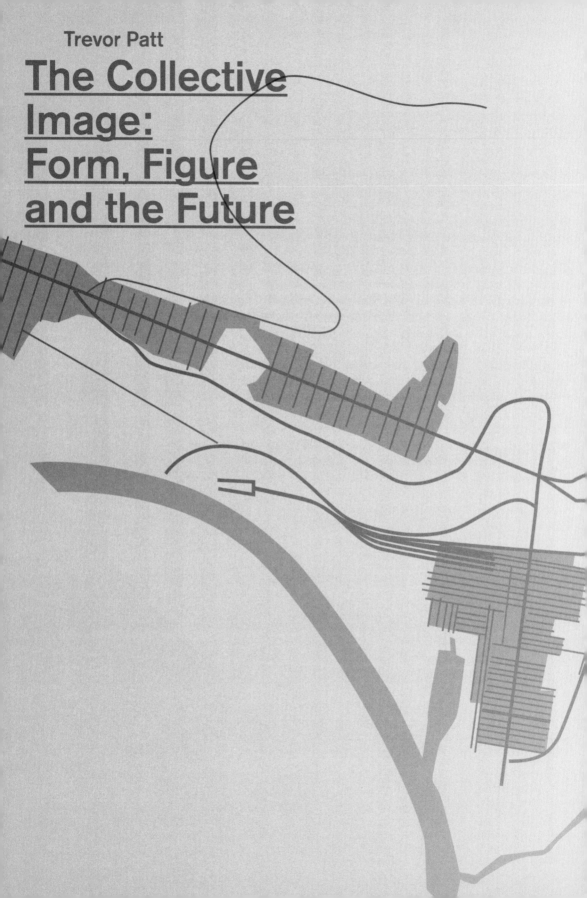

Trevor Patt

The Collective Image:
Form, Figure
and the Future

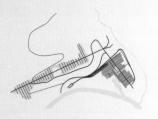

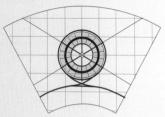

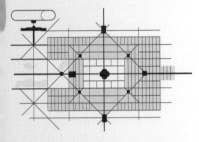

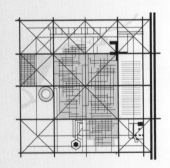

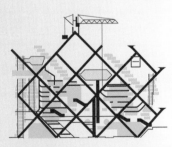

(from top) Tony Garnier, *Une Cité Industrielle*, 1917; Ebenezer Howard, *Garden City*, 1898; Le Corbusier, *Ville Contemporaine*, 1922; Frank Lloyd Wright, *Broadacre City*, 1932-1959; Peter Cook, *Plug-in City*, 1964.

An image of the future is not the same thing as a prediction. As the trajectory of innovation points to a greater and more invisible integration of parts and processes, as invention continues to push beyond the microscopic into the territory of nanotechnology, any similarity between the two grows smaller and smaller. While the contrast was perhaps less pronounced at the beginning of the twentieth century, when innovation was largely located in physical, mechanical inventions, the distinction between the serious-minded proposal and the imagery of fantastical speculation already existed. The prediction is required by definition to positively explain how something will work or what it will be; the image of the future is concerned instead with how that something will *appear*. The image asks only, "How will it seem?"

This is not to say that the image takes the easy way out. The future image is caught in a unique position between the novelty and unfamiliarity required by a scene of things-to-come and the recognizability that allows access to its content. These projective images require that they first be identified as images of the future before they can be understood. Each image of the future, like any member of a genre, relies on a history of other projective images for a set of conventions and expectations as well as a language of futurity.[1] Like the Claude glass, "the future" is both a frame which locates an image within a collection of like images, and a filter which imbues it with

1— "Every text *participates* in one or several genres, there is no genreless text … yet such participation never amounts to belonging … because of the *trait* of participation itself, because of the effect of the code and of the generic mark." Jacques Derrida, "The Law of Genre," in *Acts of Literature*, ed. Derek Attridge (New York: Routledge, 1992), 230.

those characteristics that define the type.[2] The image of the future can only exist as invention represented through a particular language.

Among the most persistent of these codes are those surrounding the city of the future: the new metropolis. The metropolis's confluence of economy, movement, communication, behavior, and technology has made it a productive subject for speculation about the future and an irresistible target for architects.[3] The metropolis motif appeared to eliminate any element of the historical city from architectural vocabulary; yet in its supposed annulment, the historical city survived as an ideal. The loss of the organic city produced a desire to subdue the frenzy of the metropolis and somehow recover the possibility of a unified city despite the sudden ineffectuality of historical authority. Seeking new guidelines for articulation and differentiation, architecture embraced the tamable logic of machines.

Architectural designs on the city of the future have thus tended to fall on the side of prediction, explanation, and organization, and have formed among themselves a fairly homogeneous model. Since being initiated in Tony Garnier's *Une cité industrielle*, the metropolis in the hands of the architect has been concerned with organizational clarity, the compartmentalization of cities by function, hierarchical traffic control, and models of rationality and efficiency. Around the same time, Ebenezer Howard wedded the city of the future to the geometric logic of Ledoux's Cité Idéale in his own *Garden Cities of Tomorrow*.[4] These principles achieved their most complete and dogmatic realization in Le Corbusier's 1925 book, *The City of Tomorrow and Its Planning,* where he proclaims that "the city of today is dying because it is not constructed geometrically," and proposes wide, straight avenues to connect the business center to the elite housing, the worker housing, and the factories, warehouses, and industry beyond.[5] The linear logic of the machine metaphor promised the possibility of tuning every aspect of the city toward optimization. Traffic loads (automobiles and even air traffic) could be predicted, budgeted, and accommodated.

These cities of the future are, however, categorically oriented against the metropolis, because they seek to counter "the intensification of nervous stimulation" intrinsic to urban experience.[6] The order enforced is a geometric order, corresponding to a placeless, stationary view of a city which is simultaneous and ahistorical. Office blocks and residential units are

2— An analogue can be drawn with another genre: the picturesque. As Rosalind Krauss revealed, the success of the picturesque image rests contradictorily on its ability to both appear original and conform to a set of guidelines. To this end, picturesque tourists searching out singular prospects often used a Claude glass, a darkly tinted mirror, to imbue the landscape with a recognizable set of picturesque effects. See Rosalind Krauss, *The Originality of the Avant-Garde and Other Modernist Myths* (Cambridge: MIT Press, 1986), 166.

3— "The Metropolis invalidates all the previous systems of articulation and differentiation that have traditionally guided the design of cities. The Metropolis annuls the previous history of architecture." See Rem Koolhaas, "Life in the Metropolis, or The Culture of Congestion," in *Architecture Theory Since 1968*, ed. K. Michael Hays (Cambridge: MIT Press, 1998), 322.

4— Sir Ebenezer Howard, *To-Morrow: A Peaceful Path to Real Reform* (London: S. Sonnenschein, 1898); released in a second edition as *Garden Cities of Tomorrow* (London: S. Sonnenschein, 1902).

5— Le Corbusier, *The City of Tomorrow and Its Planning*, trans. Frederick Etchells (Cambridge: MIT Press, 1971), 232.

6— Georg Simmel, "The Metropolis and Mental Life," in *The Sociology of Georg Simmel*, trans. Kurt Wolff (New York: Free Press, 1950), 409.

Albert Robida, *Un quartier embrouillé*
from *Le vingtième siècle: la vie
electrique*, c. 1883.

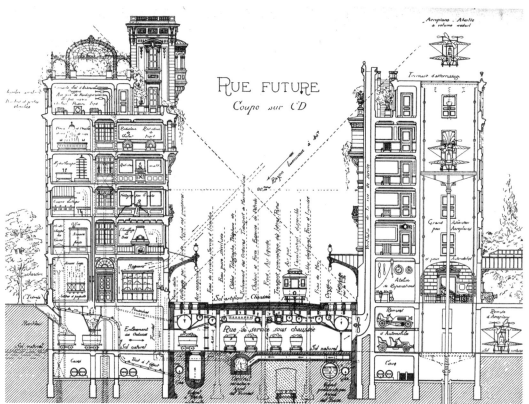

Eugène Hénard, *Rue Future*, 1910.

uniformly repeated, prismatic forms. The land between is flat and undifferentiated. This organization ignores the relationship between the city and the citizen, creating only a pretended unity. The repetition of such similar strategies reveals the limitations of an approach restricted to those aspects which lie outside any intensive encounter with the metropolis.

In contrast, the popular *image* of the metropolis is stylistically heterogeneous and visually allusive. The illustrations of Albert Robida, Moses King, and Harvey Wiley Corbett portray the metropolis of the future as a swarming and incomprehensible organism-mass that established the visual language for popular images of the future. Though no less subject to convention, they are busy and noisy, illusionistic and opaque. The massive, arching skybridges in William R. Leigh's "Great City of the Future"[7] reappear in Corbett's images and became standard forms after their recurrence in *Metropolis*. These cities, full of skyscrapers, bridges, and traffic at every level, were revisited in later futures—*Just Imagine*, *Blade Runner*, *The Fifth Element*, *Minority Report*—now covered over with a technological skin of landing pads, ports, tubes, lights,

and screens inherited from sci-fi and fantasy comics.[8] The influence of previous historical models is folded into the image and creates the history of the scene itself. Because these images do not try to illustrate (let alone effect) the constraint of a metropolis under a single organizational system, but rather exist to portray the aggregation and intensification of information, they can present an accumulated history alongside novel invention. The scene, to quote Michael Fried, causes a "dispersal [of] and resistance to any resolving hegemony."[9] Despite its heterogeneity, an identity of the city appears. By acknowledging the impossibility of constructing a static, definitive model of the metropolis's organization or explanation, the popular image is able to represent the mood of the metropolis by adopting an active and temporary viewpoint which remains comfortably in flux.[10]

This gives the image a strategic advantage over the prediction. Images are slippery but powerful; predictions, despite their technical authority, are comparatively ineffectual. Part of this weakness comes from the fact that predictions give an illusion that the metropolitan system can somehow be stepped outside of and contained. Predictions are closed and brittle constructions; any small inaccuracy is enough to render the entire prediction obsolete. Where predictions are rigid, images are agile. Rather than needing to discard or disprove previous futures, images are able to reappropriate their past

7— See his painting of *The Great City of the Future*, which accompanied Hudson Maxim, "Man's Machine-Made Millenium," *Cosmopolitan* (November 1908): 569–577.

8— This is of course an incredibly brief outline. A complete listing would include hundreds of other works and individuals from Grosz to Gibson and Giger.

9— Fried is writing about the landscape painter Claude-Joseph Vernet. See Michael Fried, *Absorption and Theatricality: Painting and Beholder in the Age of Diderot* (Berkeley: University of California Press, 1980), 136; cited in Kim Ian Michasiw, "Nine Revisionist Theses on the Picturesque," *Representations* no. 38 (Spring 1992): 88. Michasiw continues, "the effect is that of deferring rather than denying unity, of suggesting but not providing."

10— Hubert Damisch, *Skyline: The Narcissistic City* (Stanford: Stanford University Press, 2001), 12.

incarnations into fresh inspiration. Where predictions impose limits, images open connections. They instigate and capture desire in a way that allows us to access knowledge from a wide range of sources and multiple fields, requiring our collaboration with existing and emerging tropes outside of our expertise. Images can operate simultaneously within both predefined and continuously rearranging structures of knowledge.

Perhaps it is natural for an insecure profession like architecture to have favored the predictive mode. Despite (or in the face of) its need to collaborate with various disciplines, architecture has always insisted on preserving a single, authored control. Just as the modern project was predictive in its utopianism and the critical project in its didacticism, the so-called postcritical project is predictive in its own way. Though intending to build a new, more open model, postcriticality has so far fallen into the easy seduction of certainty. The recent discontent with criticality in architecture stems primarily from a feeling of constriction: a sense that the established methods available to a critical practice are now closed and closing in on the designer.[11] Not only are the methods—textuality, resistance, legibility, index, process—known from the beginning, so, it seems, are the results. As a backlash, the postcritical movement has coalesced around ideas like shape, mood, graphic, and atmosphere. In place of criticality's credo

that architecture ought to refuse or expose the ills of consumer society, these strategies are categorized as cool easiness. This misreads the cause of criticality's perceived oppressiveness. The problem is not that the system of critical operation is difficult or linguistic, but rather that it is asserted *as a system*.

The difficulty in assessing postcritical thought stems from a contradiction between the language and the methods. I think many of the impulses are correct: a decreased emphasis on representation and legibility,

11— Dave Hickey, "On Not Being Governed," *Harvard Design Magazine* no. 25 (Fall 2006/Winter 2007): 74.

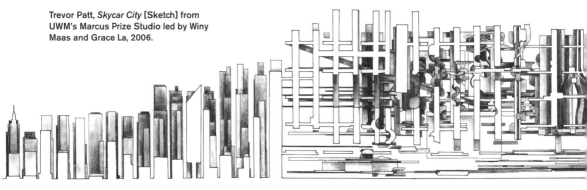

Trevor Patt, *Skycar City* [Sketch] from UWM's Marcus Prize Studio led by Winy Maas and Grace La, 2006.

dealing head-on with architecture that is (ap)percieved only in a state of distraction, and encouraging the production of new collectives and communities. If the temptation to define itself through tracts and manifestos had been resisted, these approaches could have produced a projective ground for architecture. As it is, postcritical theory is merely affecting to project from what is actually only a *prediction* of itself. Rallied around a product which fulfills the definition of postcritical rather than around the source and substance of its effects, the postcritical intention has valorized the effects. The vision of architectural production it proposes—a near throwback to classical performance[12]—is, in consequence, "brief, unverifiable, evocative rather than memorable, spectacular rather than optical, effective rather than signifying."[13]

The mistake both the critical and postcritical projects have made is naming the event beforehand and so freezing the relationship between architecture and event. As a result, the architectural proposal exists only to realize the predicted event, and is then all too quickly exhausted in self-representation. The new "projected" direction, by marrying itself too closely to criticality's equally systemic opposite, threatens to impose the same hindrances. Setting down a bullet-pointed list (it's "easier" than an essay, but no less prescriptive) of what postcritical effects would mean—as Robert Somol does in "12 Reasons to Get Back into Shape," for example—reveals

the desire to produce systematized operative logics.[14] This model backslides into the barren domain of metaphors, logos, icons, and mascots.[15] The mindset of the neccessary clean break only leads back to the dead end of predictions. The intellectual effort spent in dismantling only doubles the amount of useful information discarded.

The power of the image as a conceptual framework still remains untapped by a profession which prides itself on its powerful purveyorship of imagery. This is no small point.

12— The use of "classical" here and "didactic" earlier reference the three schema relating art to truth developed by Alain Badiou. (The third schema is romantic.) Briefly, the didactic schema states that "all truth is external to art" and is linked to Plato and dialecticism, while in the classical schema, "the purpose... of art is not in the least truth [but] involves the disposition of the passions in a transference onto semblance. Art has a therapeutic function, and not at all a cognitive or revelatory one." Classicism is associated with Aristotle and psychoanalysis. See Alain Badiou, *Handbook of Inaesthetics*, trans. Alberto Toscano (Stanford: Stanford University Press, 1998), 1–15.

13— Sylvia Lavin, "Performing the Contemporary, or: Towards an Even Newer Architecture," in *Performalism: Form and Performance in Digital Architecture*, eds. Yasha Grobman and Eran Neuman (Tel Aviv: Tel Aviv Museum of Art, 2008), 24.

14— R. E. Somol, "12 Reasons to Get Back into Shape," in *Content*, eds. OMA and Rem Koolhaas (Köln: Tashen, 2004), 86–87.

15— Somol tries to differentiate "logo" from "icon" by claiming that icons are "associated with and generally exhausted by metaphorical displacement"—though the logo examples given are also referred to metaphorically as whales, periscopes, Monopoly houses, and amoebas—within the essay "Green Dots 101," *Hunch: The Berlage Institute Report* no. 11 (Winter 2006/2007): 33.

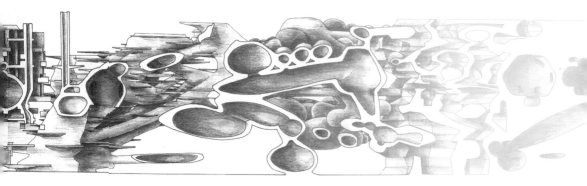

Imagery dictates the way architecture relates to its production, both through practice and communication, and to its internal dialogue. If architecture can learn to harness a method that is networked and opportunistic rather than contrary and sealed off, it will actually be able to be creative, discursively critical, *and* projective in concert.

Of course, the line between prediction and image is not so clear-cut, even in historical precedents. Some architects have been able to work both sides of this operation and to manage something of a synthesis. The drawings of Antonio Sant'Elia and his fellow futurist, Virgilio Marchi, suggest a future of highly efficient, optimized flows of people, goods, and information, but also simultaneously imply a freedom of movement and unregulated potential in an imagined city incapable of being presented in its totality.[16] The drawings of Hugh Ferriss are also notable in this regard. Even though the *Metropolis of Tomorrow* emerged from a rational delineation of the city through the exclusive influences of street grid and building code setbacks, his renderings project an extremely compelling sense of possibility which remains uninterested in the control mechanisms wielded. Similar combinations were achieved by a number of architects in the 1960s, including Constant Nieuwenhuys, Yona Friedman, Superstudio, and Archigram. At their best, they balanced aleatory movement with a regulating organization that was dynamic rather than teleological. This is why the open data networks of Archigram's *Computer City* remain superior to the predefined aesthetic kineticism of their contemporaneous *Plug-In City*. Sometimes the logic of the image is, paradoxically, betrayed by overly direct translation into imagery.

What then can we conclude about the qualities of the image? Most importantly, it is necessary to remember that the image is partial. The image engages and requires reciprocal engagement; the situation and the particulars of its deployment are active parts of its definition at any given moment. The action of the image mirrors, but does not predict, the operation of the future.[17] The image is therefore achronic, even as it grows and dies, transforms and shifts. Though generated architectural objects may be short-lived, even bound to a moment, the image persists as the qualitative ability to produce new material possibilities. There is no true "presence of absence,"[18] but simply existence in a dormant, unactivated form, or more likely, existence in an entirely different form. It is possible to capture this difference with an image because an image is itself an anexact form. Unlike

16— See Sanford Kwinter's explication of *La Citta Nuova* as a "procedural map" in *Architectures of Time: Toward a Theory of the Event in Modernist Culture* (Cambridge: MIT Press, 2001), 52–100.

17— Remember that the future itself "is a place-holder, a placebo, a no-place, but it is also a commonplace that we need to investigate in all its cultural and historical density." See Daniel Rosenberg and Susan Harding, *Histories of the Future* (Durham: Duke University Press, 2005).

18— Peter Eisenman, *Written into the Void: Selected Writings 1990–2004* (New Haven: Yale University Press, 2007), 3.

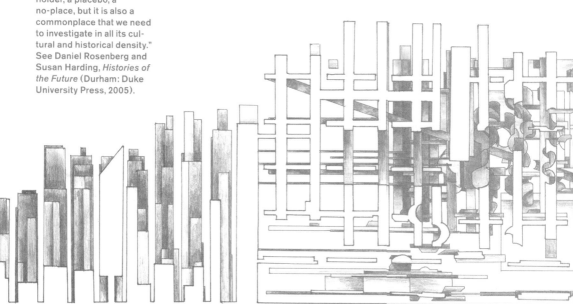

a prediction, which only supports one outcome, the image can be pressed into multiple service. The space between the image and its results is not one of linear causality. The interaction between the image and its particular interpretation or temporarily associated event can be allowed to play out in unpredictable ways. A subtractive dimension works to effect a removal of the operations from sight, and this preempts indexical reading, since as Alain Badiou reminds us, "traces can signify an event only if this event has been decided."[19] Rather, the image plays with an inversion of that expectation. By remaining undecided, it encourages speculation into the possible mechanisms hiding beneath the surface, and encourages the production of events.

We know that images are not predictions but agents. They "do something" instead of simply representing because they are not working alone. As an example, the way architectural tropes such as multilevel traffic lanes were reappropriated by makers of fictional metropoli, as images, allowed them to be reinterpreted to different ends in the chase scenes of *Blade Runner*, *The Fifth Element*,

19— Badiou, *Handbook of Inaesthetics*, 130.

and *Minority Report*. In each, a similar image of "the city of the future" is forced to interact with unique socioeconomic structures, legal systems, individual motives, and ultimately, viewer interpretations. The image is never fully codified, allowing it to be continually revisited. The image of the future is the collective sum of these vacuoles, constituting an ever-changing history, and containing within itself, through the objects it presents, a preemptive history of things-to-come. Inasmuch as the image of the future presents recognizable objects—buildings, streets, vehicles, clothing—its inner history provides some intuitions into the workings of this future. Recognizable objects mediate between the invention of the image and the sense of being-there, while at the same time they highlight the distance between the image and the present, creating another temporal frame of imagined transformation yet to be undergone by the viewer. This co-incidence of the instantaneous present, an appropriated referential past, and a projected future perfect begins to illustrate the complex incompleteness of the image and the unique demand for a reciprocated engagement it produces. There is no prescribed method of interpretation, no secret decoder ring: the image is completely reliant on the potential of, not a present-as-is or a present-as-has-become, but a present-becoming-future.

To come back to the possibility of a projective practice, Robert Somol is right to get excited about the performative speech act, where "the saying of it makes it so," because it raises the possibility of individualized actors behaving not as "descriptions or representations of this world, but establish[ing] the construction of another. In this way performatives are not subject to evaluations of falsifiability,"[20] but can instead be judged on their agency: what they can construct. If the goals of a projective practice are to instigate action and engender collective engagements with architecture, and to engage architecture with new kinds of subjects, we cannot, as designers, afford to be deterministic about how these will happen.[21] A post-event reconstruction is sufficient for a predictive formulation because it only needs to read back what was predicted, but to project forward into the future requires openness and some measure of uncertainty. We must exceed the causality that criticality relies on. This may mean that architects must forgo the creation of authored meanings in exchange for the promotion of *othered* possibilities.

The most direct way I see to move in this direction is to invert the standard architectural model of an articulated system composed of generic (inert) parts, by working instead with the specific agency of individual actors toward the production of generic (potential) networks. In doing so, architecture would commit itself to the *possibility* of fact. Architecture might become a backgrounded figure, but it would also be untethered from any predetermined form or formula. If architecture has always been experienced in a state of distraction,[22] a background-architecture might just form a new, collective but differentiated attention through its connections.

Architecture which functions like an image would be partial in the same way that an image, with only evocative suggestions, activates the existing neurons of the imagination. The capabilities of parametricism need to be reconsidered, not as a style of geometric form-making,[23] but as generic structures which can be made to work in concert with and in relation to many forces and agents.[24] As interfacial actors, parametric systems can be made to exceed the systematization that so often reduces them to a result of formal articulation,

20— Somol, "Green Dots 101," 29.

21— "In fact, it is impossible to interrogate the traces of an event except under the hypothesis of an act of naming." Badiou, *Handbook of Inaesthetics*, 130.

22— Walter Benjamin, "The Work of Art in the Age of Mechanical Reproduction" [1936], in *Illuminations*, ed. Hannah Arendt (New York: Schocken Books, 1969), 239.

23— Patrik Schumacher, "Parametricism: A New Global Style for Architecture and Urban Design," in *Architectural Design: Digital Cities* 79, no. 4 (July/August 2009): 14–23.

24— "Such a subset will ineluctably be one that no predicate can unify—an untotalizable subset, a subset that can be neither constructed nor named in the language. Such subsets are called *generic* subsets." Alain Badiou, "Philosophy and Truth," in *Infinite Thought*, eds. and trans. Oliver Feltham and Justin Clemens (London: Continuum, 2003), 48.

and can instead be employed as *effective* agents that are not exhausted in a single performance. Because the parametric is operationally generic, it can be deployed flexibly as an architectural interface *between* the mechanisms of program and client-finance structures rather than merely within their service, not by solving everything but by working alongside and with other *creative* and contradictory forces. Architecture which functions like the image would negotiate between local idiosyncrasies and cultural precedent, and between memory and organizational strategy. It would enable productive reference to precedent, but resist reduction to predetermined conclusions or quotation. This kind of architecture would address itself to a plural subject—active or distracted, critical or consumptive, rational or schizophrenic—denying only omniscience. We could say, with Barthes, that such architectural incidents would be "half-identifiable: they come from codes which are known but their combination is unique... a difference repeatable only as difference."[25] Image-architecture would preserve the individuality of actors and maintain the conditions of their participation in networks and the aspects of their multiple desires which are irreconcilable (and thus irreducible) to a system.

Forty years ago, Robert Venturi called for complexity and contradiction in architecture. Complexity has been taken up with more enthusiasm than perhaps any other subject in recent history, but all too often in a form that is unavoidably totalizing. Perhaps the day for contradiction has arrived. Let's take advantage of the exemption from "evaluations of falsifiability" and discard predictable, predictive models. A rigorous theory of architecture is not incompatible with contradiction. In fact, Michael Guggenheim suggests that the unique character of architecture is precisely its capacity to support contradictory forces and thus the impossibility of being able to be reduced to a single technology.[26] Exploring the possibilities of projective practice requires not being satisfied with the effects we already know but rather seeking the potential caught up in competing contingencies. The construction of collective images in architecture would exceed systematization. This would be a projective practice.

25— Roland Barthes, "From Work to Text," in *Image, Music, Text*, ed. and trans. Stephen Heath (New York: Hill and Wang, 1978), 159.

26— Michael Guggenheim, "Mutable Immobiles: Building Conversation as a Problem of Quasi-Technologies," in *Urban Assemblages: How Actor-Network Theory Changes Urban Studies*, eds. Thomas Bender and Ignacio Farias (London: Routledge, 2009), 161–178, and "Building Memory: Architecture, Networks and Users," *Memory Studies* 2, no. 1 (2009): 39–53.

RUE FUTURE

Coupe sur CD

Aeroplane. Abeille
à volume réduit

Terrasse d'atterrissage

Rayon lumineux à 45°

Rayon lumineux

20.00 Mètres

Grand   Ascenseur
  pour   Aéroplanes

et pour   Automobiles

Voûte dalle
Nettoyage par le vide
Appel des voyageurs
Air comprimé
Service d'incendie
Eau de rivière
Eau pure stérilisée
Câbles - Télégraphe - Téléphone etc
Enlèvement des Ordures
Transport de Marchandises
Chaleur et Force
Essence de Pétrole
Froid - Air liquide
Transport pneumatique des lettres, Petits Paquets
Air pur
Canalisation disponible
Câbles électriques - Force et lumière
Eau de Mer
Orgueur
Nettoyage par le vide

Ventilation de la rue de service

Atelier
de Réparations

Remises

d'Automobiles

Cave

Sol artificiel   Chaussée

Rue de service sous chaussée

Sol naturel

Airtight—

A conversation between Philippe Rahm and Esther Choi

Translated by Suzanne Ernst and Ana Manao

Esther Choi— I experienced your installation *Interior Weather*, designed for the Canadian Center for Architecture in Montreal in 2006, and like others, was lured by its refined aesthetic resolution. While the subject matter of the installation engaged in an architectural discourse by questioning the discipline's assumptions about form, function and materiality, its use of materials and spatial configuration also seemed to address the adjacent field of art installation practices. *Interior Weather* conjured very specific references in an art historical context, ranging from minimalism to the milieu of perceptual-light experimentalists such as Dan Flavin, Robert Irwin, Olafur Eliasson, et alia.

This aspect of your work—the way in which it straddles disciplinary boundaries—allows for it to operate on multiple disciplinary and discursive registers. How would you define your position as an architect working in this manner, and could you discuss your own process of formulating projects within museum-based contexts in a way that clarifies the relationship of your work to the discourses and practices of installation art? How do you feel the particular context within which the work is created (i.e. in a museum) defines or affects the meaning of the work as both a speculative architectural project and an artistic construct? How does working in a museum further the possibilities for projective and speculative architectural practices? The way you have shaped your practice leads me to wonder whether one strategy for projective practice would be engaging in an explicit merging or appropriation of languages from related disciplines.

Philippe Rahm— In my opinion, the question about the relationship between art and architecture can find relevance only at the moment when a language is invented. Architecture becomes art when it has invented a language, just as art becomes art when it has invented a language. This is why I am so interested in Aldo Rossi, Peter Eisenman, Robert Venturi and Le Corbusier, because they have, even before realizing buildings, invented a language. They have transformed the manner of thinking about space; they have altered paradigms. They have rethought "the root of architecture," and when there is this invention of language, there is art.

The museum is the place, more than a book or an article, where we can work and express and present a new language as architects. But obviously the tools of an architect are not the same as those used by an artist or a musician.

Those of an architect must always involve the real and the physical. If a graphic artist's concern is "representation," the architect's concern is "presentation": that is to say, the concern with pure presence in space, immediate and present. Therefore the CCA exhibition was an installation that sought possible functions for climatic data measured in real time. That project marked for me the beginning of questioning the origin of typologies in architecture. It enabled me to put into question the relation between form and function, and especially allowed me to begin to imagine new typologies in terms of climate. My goal was to renew architectural language through a slippage of the visible toward the invisible and the tectonic toward the climatic, where space is qualified in terms of new paradigms such as light, temperature and humidity. It amused me to call "typology," that spearhead of postmodernism, into question, but I also think that it is necessary to reconsider the question of function in terms of the climatic stakes of today.

In his letter to Pope Leon X at the beginning of the sixteenth century, the painter Raphaël described the specificity of technical architectural representation by differentiating it from that of the painter: the plan for the architect, the perspective for the painter. Thus Raphaël, like Alberti, expressed the distinction between architect and painter by asserting the drawing of the plan for the architect, and limiting the use of the perspective as the tool of the artist.

It seems important to us today to return to this fundament: to return to the plan, to its drawing, to return to work upstream of images, to work in the matrix of architectural form and programming, at the heart of its codes and language. The history of architecture is marked by critical moments where we understand that the return of the plan, the essential architectural representation, is necessary because it allows the fundamental requestioning of the language of architecture. Asking fundamental questions of the architectural language seems then like a kind of necessary diet in periods where academicism triumphs and masks the real stakes of the moment. Academicism is a period of development; it is a multiplication of projects and perspectives derived from the same plan-matrix, and from the same thought that we forget to put into question.

Le Corbusier's return to the plan in 1921 (in *Towards an Architecture*) was therefore made necessary in a historical situation where the same academic grammar was being used for a multitude of architecture projects which were being produced without any investigation into the language of architecture, despite the emergence of notable new construction techniques, such as steel and reinforced concrete. The "free plan" was the most extraordinary architectural intervention at the beginning of the twentieth century, because in fully accepting the plastic potentials and programming of reinforced concrete, and in simply disjoining the form of space from the carrying structure, Le Corbusier invented a new type of architectural plan capable of generating new architectural and urban forms while encouraging the development of new uses and new modes of living. This is why the concept of the "architectural project" is a trap. It does not question the essence of architecture, relying instead on a predefined language while luring us with a false richness of expression based on a diversity of appearances, which are, in reality, simple consequences of a multiplicity of contexts. I prefer the idea of a "project of the architecture project" or even the "architecture of the project," which questions architecture like language and rethinks the typology of the plan in the process of architectural creation. Architecture is the invention of typologies and the creation of plans. When it becomes an "architecture of the project," or an "invention of a language," it rises to the level of art. The perspective can perhaps follow afterward.

Our current work is strictly to try to define new typologies: to invent new plans and cuts formed from the stakes and current technical means of reality widened by the knowledge of today. The development of life sciences, molecular biology and genetics on the one side, and atmospheric problems caused by global warming on the other encourage a shift, or more precisely, a widening of the spectrum of reality, that extends the visible toward the invisible, the macroscopic toward the microscopic and climatic, the inorganic toward the organic, and the biological toward the meteorological. Our work is to formulate new typologies that can exist between the meteorological and the physiological while articulating air currents, the displacement of steam, ventilation rates, acoustic pressures, temperatures, breathing, perspiration and nutrients.

EC— I'd like to unpack your phrase, "a new language," and examine two things: first, what this phrase may imply in a disciplinary or discursive sense, and second, how this may connect to notions of architectural and aesthetic efficacy.

The tenets of minimalism were largely influenced by
architectural ideas, materials and fabrication processes; they were not *solely* a reaction to internal
conversations concerning modernist sculpture within the
art world. Minimalism introduced a seemingly "new" language of spatial and temporal immanence into the discourse of art, but similar theories of spatiality were,
of course, floating around much earlier in architectural
and art historical discourses. You referred to "presentation" as being an architect's concern, but in this particular instance (and in many others), we can trace the
longstanding and incestuous cross-pollination of ideas
between art and architecture. Likewise, on a purely formal level, your installations make reference to formal
and aesthetic precedents existing in postwar and contemporary art practices. Although you assert that the
framework for your practice is specifically architectural
in its concerns, should not some acknowledgement still
be made to the adjacent movements that have profoundly
affected architectural thought and practice, even on
"merely" a formal level?

Shifting gears, I would like to concentrate on the issue
of scale and discuss its effects in your work. The movement toward the microscopic raises interesting questions
related to how the effects of your work are biochemi-
cally received and interpreted by audiences. Your interest in altering chemical or hormonal states through the
formation of climatic and alchemic atmospheres models an
architecture of invisible conditions that is understood
as an internal, neurological and affective state within
the body. Perhaps a new language could be located in neu-
roaesthetic strategies which challenge previous constitu-
tions of *architectural effect* by proposing new registers
and sensorial modalities for *architectural efficacy*. You
mentioned that academicism can mask the real stakes of
the moment, but for me, the real stakes have not yet been
discussed. How could aesthetic and spatial experiences
(in art or architecture) serve to *challenge* the body's
perception or negotiation of its surroundings, and in
turn reshape the sphere of one's subjective experience?
The question of legibility is crucial here: how does your
work address issues of control and *agency* on the part of
your subjects? Is an armature provided whereby participants may respond to your work by actively contributing
to the formation of their experiences?

PR— If we want to know the essence of architecture, we
finally have to return to our "endothermic" condition:

the necessity of maintaining a body temperature at 37°
Celsius. Architecture exists because of the enzymes necessary for the biochemical reactions of the human metabolism. Present by billions in our bodies, these molecules
can work in an optimal way only at a temperature between
35 and 37.6°C. Humans have to maintain constant physical
temperature independent of the outside temperature. For
that purpose, they compose various mechanisms of physiological thermoregulation and external protections such as
clothing and/or shelter. This means that architecture is
not autonomous: it is simply one of a range of means to
maintain our optimal temperature. It is a response to a
steep decline or increase of the body temperature, along
with, for example, vasodilatation mechanisms, sweating,
thirst or muscular contractions. These responses develop
from nature to artifice, microscopic to macroscopic,
biochemical to meteorological, and digestive to urban,
in the interstices between physiological determinism
and pure cultural freedom. In this context, architecture appears as a bigger method of vasoconstriction, or,
conversely, eating appears as a smaller variant of architecture. In the end architecture is nothing more than an
exogenous change and a kind of artificial thermogenesis
or thermolysis.

From an anthropological point of view, when we think that
we are too cold or too warm, we find the cause outside
of ourselves, in an inadequate outside climate at an
atmospheric level. We try to make this outside climate
comfortable by correcting it—that is the origin and the
mission of architecture. In reality, the first signs of
architecture are physiological and totally internal and
autonomous; we perspire if it is too warm or shiver if
it is too cold. These are the first responses to a rise
or a reduction of body temperature due to an unfavor-
able thermal environment. Then, in the simplest way, the
most rudimentary gestures follow: the urge to drink if
it is too warm, in order to lower temperature by evapo-
ration, or to eat if it is too cold, to launch the com-
bustion process of nutrients which will produce some
metabolic heat. After these endogenous corrections, if
the body still fails to compensate for the temperature of
the outside environment, the range of geographical corrections develops, and these include migration, clothing
and architectural construction. To paraphrase Vitruvius,
architecture in cold countries or winter appears as an
increased, exogenous thermogenesis which is outside the
body, while architecture in warm countries or summer

presents itself as an exteriorized thermolysis. Both artificially correct the uncomfortable parts of nature.

It might seem surprising to go back to these basic reasons and means for architecture, but the problem of global warming suddenly brings the climatic responsibilities of architecture back to mind. Architects of today have to understand how we can limit energy consumption and the production of greenhouse gas. We advocate for a densification of the city and for a concentration of functions to limit energy wasted in transport. But can we not also experiment with less heavy, less present, almost homeopathic architecture which nevertheless still retains the ambition of climatic correction? We would like to investigate sensitive zones closer to the body, at the limit of our skin. Let's not make a mistake! If the architectural search consists merely of finding ways to save energy and fight global warming, it misses the concurrent opportunity for discovering new modes of housing and kinds of spatial compositions where scales mix and architecture becomes as structural as food and sweating.

EC— On the one hand, characterizing architecture as a response to the human body's need to maintain its endothermic condition presents a refreshingly "realistic" program for the discipline. It positions architecture as a broader practice connected to the larger forces in the world (climate, environment, human survival) while channeling its various outputs and inputs to respond to the body's homeostatic activities. But doesn't this position also diminish the complex and multifaceted nature of human beings and our ability for self-reflexive thought? While we need to take our corporeal needs into account within architectural thought and action, surely we cannot divorce this reality from the cultural, economic and social forces that shape our lives. For example, in his book *Parables for the Virtual*, the philosopher Brian Massumi discusses the bifurcated relationship between our formulations of the "the body" as understood through a lens of corporeality, affect and sensation, and the notions of "the subject" understood through poststructuralist cultural theory.[1] I feel strongly that we have a responsibility to envision how architecture may foster a more nuanced relationship between the physiological *and* the larger forces that shape subjectivity. How this may occur is, of course, an enormous question.

1— Brian Massumi, *Parables for the Virtual: Movement, Affect Sensation* (Durham and London: Duke University Press, 2002), 2-7.

In many ways, framing "the body" on a physiological
level is similar to the universalism of the plan, and the
formulation of "the subject" is akin to the locational
specificity of the perspective. Both the plan and the
perspective offer two limited notations of experiential
knowledge that are not easily reconcilable. A plan offers
a detached viewpoint; its authoritative and universal
"objectivity" masks the intensities of the sets of relations it presents. Similarly, a perspectival view also
presents restrictions in its fixed gaze; its sense of
proportion is determined from a limited position. Perhaps
like both the plan and the perspective, previous methods
of addressing "the body" or "the subject" in architecture
have been overly reductive, rendering the two as incompatible despite the fact that they may be articulating
the same complex experience. For example, the critical
project presented the subject as a discursive body capable of performing acts of linguistic or psychoanalytic
signification, while ignoring its sensory and physiological dimensions. If today we respond by stripping
our understanding of the body down to its physiological
aspects, we simply postpone another resurfacing of the
linguistic determinism we seek to exceed.

Instead, perhaps we need to concentrate on formulating a more nuanced notion of an architectural program in
which sensation and subjectivity are not positioned as
at odds with each other. So the question is, how might
we envision an architecture capable of reinforcing both
the physiological and the sensorial to promote new modes
of human activity? Could architecture's response to our
corporeality engender new forms of qualitative experience that in turn could transform the realms of the
social and the cultural? In light of the 2010 earth-
quake in Haiti, where poorly made buildings contributed
to a horrendous number of victims, it would be a gross
understatement to posit that it is our responsibility as
practitioners and thinkers to refresh our architectural
vocabulary and imagine how architecture might fulfill
the physiological to enact change in resonant ways. To
(re)turn to any universal standpoint is to negate the
reality that human beings are faced with dire economic
and social inequalities. I cannot help but think of the
situation in Haiti as a wake-up call for us to reexamine
the discipline's fundamental attitudes toward the body
and our varied subjectivities.

Marrikka Trotter

Re-relational Architecture, or, the Glass House

"Art requires a breath of atmosphere to enable it to exist. If it is reared in a hot-house, it is only a curiosity, an amusement, or an object of study for the privileged few. Imagine a landlord building a magnificent conservatory, and devoting all his means and employing all the labour at his disposal in raising the rarest plants in that conservatory, but letting thistles and briers cover his fields; should we not rather see the conservatory destroyed and the land producing fine woods, harvests and vintages? Our position as regards architecture in this country is something like that of such a landlord; we have a magnificent conservatory, but too many thistles in its neighborhood. The life of this art, which was formerly diffused throughout our land, is concentrated in a conservatory heated and cultivated at great expense; yet after all we should certainly prefer to take our walks in groves flourishing in the open air than beneath foliage protected by glass."

—Eugène-Emmanuel Viollet-le-Duc, Lecture XVI[1]

1— Eugène-Emmanuel Viollet-le-Duc, "Lecture XVI," *Lectures on Architecture*, Vol. II, trans. Benjamin Bucknall (London: Sampson Low, Marston, Searle and Rivington, 1881), 231. [Published in French as *Entretiens sur l'architecture* in 1872.]

Philip Johnson, Glass House,
New Canaan, Connecticut, 1949.

When we discuss the limits of architecture today, we confront an enduring consensus that architecture requires separation from adjacent fields in order to maintain disciplinary integrity. Contradictorily, this consensus was itself both a consequence and an index of a particular kind of interpenetration between design and outside influences. The framing of architecture as a formal inquiry within the constraints of commissioned works was a construct that simplified and incentivized a particular set of socioeconomic, political and ecological circumstances which have since been lost in the changeful flows of time. The contingency revealed by our contemporary circumstances demands that the ataraxic production of architectural images and objects be replaced by participation in the cultivation of a shared, entropic and finite mass of organic and inorganic life. Yet, before we can adjust our paradigms, we must confront our history.

In the middle of the fifteenth century, when Leon Battista Alberti split architecture into the conceptualization of lineaments and the selection of matter, he was seeking to codify the nascent profession and persona of the architect in a way which both recaptured the conjectured nobility of classical antiquity and reconciled with the fiscal logistics of the Renaissance.[2] The professionalization of architectural practice was a way of separating "graceful order"[3] from the viral technological and aesthetic achievement of the medieval Masonic guilds, which diffused architectural, socioeconomic, political and ecological activities into a common, synthetic landscape.[4] For

Alberti and his contemporaries, this Gothic tangle of material and conceptual was no longer useful. In the Renaissance, without the marketable service of a reasoning mind fashioning *concinnitas* from abstract Vitruvian elements, architecture had no economic value.[5] It is no coincidence that the modern profession of architecture developed together with cadastral maps. The mechanical reduction of the landscape to legible and taxable property was symbiotic with Medici and Vatican commissions of works of art and architecture from celebrity individuals for private enjoyment and ownership.[6] What was once "common" was also bisected into "public" and "private" even within the interior of newly privatized

2— "Building… consists of lineaments and matter, the one the product of thought, the other of Nature; the one requiring the mind and the power of reason, the other dependent on preparation and selection." Alberti, *On the Art of Building in Ten Books*, trans. Joseph Rykwert, Neil Leach and Robert Tavernor (Cambridge: MIT Press, 1988), Prologue (Rykwert 5).

3— Alberti, I.1 (Rykwert 7).

4— See Alain Erland-Brandenburg, *The Cathedral: The Social and Architectural Dynamics of Construction*, trans. Martin Thorn (Cambridge: Cambridge University Press, 1994), and Henry Kraus's classic description of Gothic architectural processes, *Gold Was the Mortar: The Economics of Cathedral Building* (London: Routledge and Kegan Paul, 1979).

Andrea Palladio, Facade of San
Francesco della Vigna, Venice, Italy, 1564.

5— Alberti states that beauty is ultimately both the best justification for the economic cost of building and the most enduring protection for the physical, public evidence of private expenditure. "More noble is beauty, therefore, and it must be sought most eagerly by anyone who does not wish what he owns to seem distasteful. What remarkable importance our ancestors, men of great prudence, attached to it is shown by the care they took that their legal, military, and religious institutions—indeed, the whole commonwealth—should be much embellished; and by their letting it be known that if all these institutions, without which man could scarce exist, were to be stripped of their pomp and finery, their business would appear insipid and shabby…. What other human art might sufficiently protect a building to save it from human attack? … No other means is as effective in protecting a work from damage and human injury as is dignity and grace of form. All care, all diligence, all financial consideration must be directed to ensuring that what is built is useful, commodious, yes—but also embellished and wholly graceful, so that anyone seeing it would not feel that the expense might have been invested better elsewhere." Alberti VI.2 (Rykwert 155–156).

6— See Roger J. P. Kain and Elizabeth Baigent, *The Cadastral Map in the Service of the State: A History of Property Mapping* (Chicago: Chicago University Press, 1992), and also James C. Scott, "Nature and Space," in *Seeing Like a State: How Certain Schemes to Improve the Human Condition Have Failed* (New Haven: Yale University Press, 1998), 11–52.

architecture itself: both Alberti and Andrea Palladio gave careful attention to this delineation within domestic space.[7] In a sense, such divisions were a natural co-progression with an increasingly bifurcated world, where the boundary between St. Thomas Aquinas's spiritual form and corporeal matter—existing simultaneously yet separately—was hardlined as precisely as possible in the paper-thinness of works like Palladio's facade for San Francesco della Vigna.[8] The commodification of the landscape and the distinction between mind and "the contagion of matter" thus also found expression in the form and practice of architecture, transformed from diffuse edification into the private exchange of taste between courtier-architect and patron. In the Renaissance, architectural beauty became a contractual relationship focused on the accumulation of pleasure. The codification of architectural composition and ornament permitted the efficient exchange of this pleasure, and was therefore a natural part of the socio-economic compartmentalization of expertise and taste into more easily utilized categories.

There was now an inside and an outside to architecture.[9]

Seventeenth-century scientists proceeded to invent ways of understanding the environment in a manner that was as codified as architectural convention. The cross-pollination between art and the natural sciences occurred as a fluid exchange: while Isaac Newton formulated what would eventually become a mechanical model of the universe, Christopher Wren lectured in astronomy, experimented with meteorology and wrestled with the pressing issue of how to measure longitude at sea—areas of baroque discovery which pushed western Europe's striation of space far out into the former formlessness of the ocean and the atmosphere. Whereas Renaissance treatise-writers had advised the imitation of nature and compared architectural elements to anatomical components,[10] baroque natural science was eager

7— See, for example, Alberti's discussion in book 5.1–2 (Rykwert 119–121) of his treatise, and Palladio's similar injunctions in book II.2 of *I Quattro Libri dell'Architettura* in Andrea Palladio, *The Four Books on Architecture*, trans. Robert Tavernor and Richard Schofield (Cambridge: MIT Press, 2002), 77–78.

8— St. Thomas Aquinas, *De Ente et Essentia* (Cologne: Heinrich Quentell, c. 1489). The facade's nearly flat, drawing-like aspect inscribed an exact threshold between the mercantile transactions of the Venetian city and the spiritual volume of the Church. I owe the understanding that this *thin* quality of Palladio's design is a remarkable attribute that deserves theoretical attention to Erika Naginski.

9— Alberti is overt about this way of approaching architecture: he states that his inquiry is "into the inner nature of building" I.1 (Rykwert 7).

10— See, for example, Alberti III.7–10 (Rykwert 71–75), VII.4 (Rykwert 197), and I.10 (Rykwert 25), III.14 (Rykwert 86), and IX.5 (Rykwert 301–305).

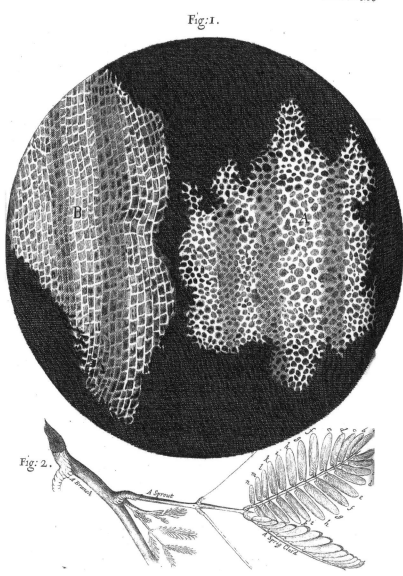

Robert Hooke, *Hooke's observations of the cellular structure of cork and a sprig of Sensible (Sensitive) Plant*, 1665.

to imitate architecture: Peter Sloterdijk has asserted that Robert Hooke appropriated the medieval architectural term "cell" to describe the interior particulate matter of life itself.[11] No longer was architecture to be thought of in terms of bones and muscles appropriated from biology, but rather bones and muscles were to be thought of in terms of units appropriated from architecture. The codification of architecture facilitated the cadastral tabulation of everything else.

It was only a matter of time before architecture and nature were re-related, not as common and interconnected in an *a priori* way, but rather as two co-locations for the exercise of artifice. Robert Morris, the principal articulator of British early-eighteenth-century architectural thought, was thus able to advance a notion of site selection which went further than that of Alberti or Palladio, or after them, Serlio or Vignola. Morris moved from nature as a *model* for the organic composition of architecture to nature as part of the material available for the compositional *extent* of architecture, advising architects to "blend Art and Nature together" to create maximum delight for the client.[12] He classified landscapes as either *grave*, to be complemented by the Doric order, *jovial*, to be complemented by the Ionic order, or *charming*, to be complemented by the Corinthian order.[13] For Morris and his contemporaries, the land could now be visually coded by deploying the appropriate architectural device.[14] Architecture made the privately improved, owned or simply glimpsed landscape an aesthetic encounter, and facilitated the relocation of its value accordingly.[15] The domain of architecture had expanded.

11— Peter Sloterdijk, "Cell Block, Egosphere, Self-Container," trans. Daniela Fabricus, *Log* 10 (Summer/Fall 2007): 92. See also Robert Hooke, *Micrographia: or, Some Physiological Descriptions of Minute Bodies Made by Magnifying Glasses, with Observations and Inquiries Thereupon* [1665] (New York: Dover Publications, 1961), 111–116.

12— Robert Morris, "Lecture V," *Lectures on Architecture Consisting of Rules Founded upon Harmonick and Arithmetical Proportions in Building, Design'd as an Agreeable Entertainment for Gentlemen: And More Particularly Useful to All Who Make Architecture, or the Polite Arts, Their Study* (London: R. Sayer, 1759 and 1736), 63–71. Morris was indebted to the Shaftesbury ideal of the "virtuoso"—someone who through "inward development of private morality" learned to construct "the outward harmony and order of the universe." See Harry Francis Mallgrave, ed., *Architectural Theory: An Anthology from Vitruvius to 1870* (Malden, MA: Blackwell Publishing Ltd., 2006), 95.

13— Robert Morris, *An Essay Upon Harmony as It Relates Chiefly to Situation and Building* (London: R. Sayer, 1739), 31–38.

14— Nevertheless, the curious confusion about the proper place of architecture continued apace. Blondel grouped architecture with agriculture in his *L'Architecture française*, while his writings were themselves grouped by Diderot and the editors of the French Encyclopedia under mathematics. See Kevin Harrington, *Changing Ideas on Architecture in the Encyclopédie, 1750–1776* (Ann Arbor: UMI Research Press, 1981), 7; 11.

15— David Leatherbarrow has argued that Morris points to an important shift in the understanding of architecture's relationship to larger flows by creating reciprocity between architectural order and the existing characteristics of a landscape; architecture had become an image which simultaneously turned the landscape into an image as well. See David Leatherbarrow, "Architecture and Situation: A Study of the Architectural Writings of Robert Morris," *The Journal of the Society of Architectural Historians* 44, no. 1 (March 1985): 48–59.

The aesthetes of the nineteenth century were able to remove architecture to the realm of the collectible—an object to be viewed through glass if not itself placed under glass.[16] The

popular Claude glass, a device which changed landscape formations and architectural objects alike into a picturesque aesthetic experience, required its users to turn their backs to the landscape. As Hugh Sykes Davies remarked, this artifact was "very typical of their attitude to Nature that such a position should have seemed desirable."[17] Landscape and architecture literally became the background for the aesthetic experience of the individual; what had been suggested as architecture's role by the writings of Robert Morris a century before was achieved instead in general attitude. Architecture, which had been first the separate intellectual *imitation* of nature, then the *model* for the codification of nature itself, and afterward the *device* through which both nature and humans could be commoditized, was now itself

16— Indeed, Joseph Paxton's Crystal Palace placed architecture in exactly this position: even Pugin's expansive vision of a revived Gothic vernacular was fit neatly into one of its bays. See Rosemary Hill, *God's Architect: Pugin and the Building of Romantic Britain* (London: Allen Lane, 2007), 453–470.

17— Hugh Sykes Davis, *Wordsworth and the Worth of Words*, ed. John Kerrigan and Jonathan Wordsworth (Cambridge: Cambridge University Press, 1986), 223.

one of the myriad elements which could be foraged for individual visual enjoyment. It was no longer a conceptual mechanism distinct from and acting upon the landscape, but rather a feature of a completely domesticated tableau that included human and nonhuman activity as equal artifice. It ceased to be its own interior and protected space and instead occupied a wider construct of optical effect.

Following the destruction at the dawn of the twentieth century, when it became clear that the atmosphere could no longer be the picturesque background for individual visual experience but was, in fact, capable of becoming viscerally poisonous, Viollet-le-Duc's greenhouse was shattered.[18] The early 1900s proved that the position of architecture *vis à vis* its reciprocally contingent flows was very much up in the air. During the early Soviet experiments of architects such as Konstantin Melnikov and the bureaucratic and architectural collaborations of Red Vienna and Wagnerian Berlin, it seemed possible that architecture must be and should be once again diffused from the place of privileged study it had occupied into the wider life of the population.[19]

Nevertheless, the quick regrowth and expansion of industry, banking, homeownership and families in the United States after WWII created political and cultural room for the renewed segregation of architectural aesthetics. Philip Johnson had already laid the groundwork for this task almost single-handedly with his importation of the "International Style" to the Museum of Modern Art in 1932, an act which reestablished architecture as an object within the larger interior of connoisseurship by simply treating it as such.

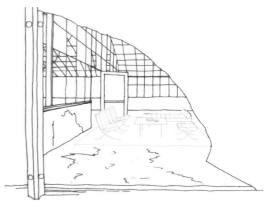

18— This was literally the case in England, where Joseph Paxton's Great Conservatory, at Chatsworth, was demolished in 1920. It had required not only enormous amounts of coal to regulate the temperature of its exotic plants, but also ten workers to maintain the facility daily; the exigencies of war had made both contingencies impossible to maintain, and the plants had all perished. See the account of the Duchess of Devonshire in her *The Garden at Chatsworth* (London: Frances Lincoln Limited, 1999), 92–98.

19— See Eve Blau, *The Architecture of Red Vienna* (Cambridge: MIT Press, 1999), and Jean-Louis Cohen, "The Misfortunes of the Image: Melnikov in Paris 1925: Architecture and Photography," in *Architectureproduction: Revisions 2*, eds. Beatriz Colomina and K. Michael Hays (Princeton: Princeton Architectural Press, 1988), 101–121.

Barry Bergdoll has suggested that Johnson might have himself redrawn Mies van der Rohe's plans of the Tugendhat House and the Barcelona Pavilion to remove "wiggly" nature; certainly Johnson sanctioned the erasure of Mies's own desire to situate his architecture in the larger context of "the unfolding of life."[20] Later, by appropriating his own land as "very expensive wallpaper" and by offering a fictional decoding of his design process for the Glass House through a series of precedents which presented architectural history and *all experience* as formal material available for appropriation,[21] Johnson reinscribed the territorial boundary from which architecture had been leaking. His design was divorced from the socioeconomic, political and ecological except as internal historical references to the residues these forces had impressed on the codes of architectural form and effect in the past. Johnson situated architecture within the space of curation; the discipline which had, in the time of the eighteenth-century Salon, provided the protective enclosure for art could now be displayed in model scale within the confines of the museum.[22] This is

20— Barry Bergdoll, lecture at Harvard GSD Symposium "The Return of Nature: The Sublime Plan" (Cambridge, MA), November 17, 2009. The quotation of Mies is from Fritz Neumeyer, *The Artless Word: Mies van der Rohe on the Building Art* [1928] (Cambridge: MIT Press, 1991), 301.

21— Including the infamous "burned-out village" which continues to haunt the discourse on Johnson. See, for instance, Kazys Varnelis, "'We Cannot Not Know History': Philip Johnson's Politics and Cynical Survival," *Journal of Architectural Education* 49, no. 2 (November 1995): 92–104.

22— For the seminal discussion of the Enlightenment admission of a "public" to the private (architectural) interior of art through the device of the Paris Salon, see Thomas Crow, *Painters and Public Life in Eighteenth-Century Paris* (New Haven: Yale University Press, 1985). There are several recent and much-needed discussions of Philip Johnson's role in defining the position of architecture vis-à-vis other forces and discourses. See, for instance, Mark Jarzombek's "Working Out Johnson's Role in History," in *Philip Johnson: The Constancy of Change*, ed. Emmanuel J. Petit (New Haven: Yale University Press, 2009), 234–239.

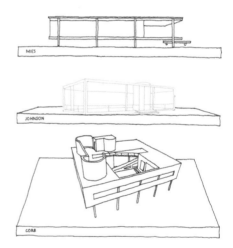

not to say that Johnson's move was a perni-cious or arbitrary act of miniaturization and relocation. In reality, the sustainable space for a delineated disciplinary architectural interior had collapsed and could not be recaptured.[23] Architecture as an autonomous aesthetic practice and discourse could henceforth exist only as a guest within other spaces which had not yet lost their larger socioeconomic, politi-cal and ecological value. But art is also not immune to larger shifts.

Today, the supposed interiority of the aesthetic dimension in both art and archi-tecture has been challenged not by their own foregrounding but by the rise from the background of everything else. That there is no such thing as autonomy truly separate from its larger context has now become a near-ubiquitous understanding. The support structures of economics, culture, ecologi-cal balance and politics required to nurture aesthetic development are on the move today as they were during the 1960s and 1970s, at the turn of the twentieth century, and at many other times in history, pooling here and there in rapid geopolitical and financial eddies. The reassuring stiffness of cadastral simplification is eroding in the unavoidable context of con-tingent survival. The future of architecture will not look like its past, unless it has no future beyond a minute extension of its present, and so we must reexamine the past for alternative sets of relationships. Let's rewind.

While other architects were seeking to codify architecture within linguistic limits, Christopher Alexander and Buckminster Fuller were interested in the autopoietic propaga-tion of architectural activity into the commu-nity and the environment at large. Alexander

believed that *living* architecture—much like J. S. Haldane's single, completed organism of a living lung and the atmosphere—required con-tinuous and reciprocal coupling with its politi-cal, socioeconomic and ecological contexts.[24] At the same time, Fuller asserted that "the human is not an accidental onlooker ... but an essential syntropic function of Universe."[25] Likewise, only one year before Philip Johnson began his curatorial project, Frank Lloyd Wright observed that the circumference of the architectural discipline was shifting in response to the changing pressures of out-side forces.[26] In 1910, Wright stipulated that vernacular "folk-buildings" were more fertile exemplars than anything that existed within the architectural canon proper because they responded not to the interior vocabulary of academic architecture, but to the external con-ditions of place, habit and lifeworld.[27] He sug-gested that "a revival, not of the Gothic style but of the Gothic spirit," would result in a "liv-ing" architecture, "until all these borrowed gar-ments now being cut over to fit by Academies are cast off, having served only to hide the pitiful nakedness of a moment when Art became detached, alien to the lives of people: academic. An affair for museums, of institutes and standardized universities—weaknesses only exaggerated by the facilities afforded by modern machinery."[28] Wright was the first to see architecture as a cofragile sphere, to use Peter Sloterdijk's terminology.[29] He sought architecture as part of a "whole" assembled as an aggregation of "individual units ... not yoked from outside in bondage, but united by spirit from the inside with the right to freely move, resist aggression or invasion, but only each in its own sphere."[30] Wright wanted to move past

23— Philip Johnson's own Ghost House relives this situation. Composed of chain link, it is nothing but an armature for the vines which grow over it and give it form—a small, weak version of the eighteenth century's astonishing Green House in the Gardens at Wrest. In Johnson's own end-narrative, architecture has become form so evacuated of function that it is only a puff of remnant meaning.

24— Marrikka Trotter, "The Infinite Unfolding of Christopher Alexander: Synthesis, Ghosts and Other Unbound Points in the Recent Architectural Past" (MDesS Thesis, Harvard University Graduate School of Design, 2009).

25— This was one of his fourteen concepts modeled on Woodrow Wilson's fourteen points. Buckmister Fuller, "Letter to Doxiadis," *Main Currents in Modern Thought* 25; no. 4 (March-April 1969), 90, quoted in Alden Hatch, *Buckminster Fuller: At Home in the Universe* (New York: Crow Publishers, 1974), 235.

26— Frank Lloyd Wright, "To the Young Man in Architecture," 1931 lecture at the Art Institute of Chicago, published in *Frank Lloyd Wright: Writings and Buildings*, ed. Edgar Kaufmann and Ben Raeburn (New York: Horizon Press, 1960), 233.

27— Frank Lloyd Wright, "The Sovereignty of the Individual in the Cause of Architecture," *Ausgeführte Bauten und Entwürfe* (Berlin: Wasmuth, 1910), 5.

28— Ibid., 7.

29— Peter Sloterdijk, *Sphären III: Schäume* (Frankfurt: Suhrkamp Verlag, 2004), Prologue.

30— Ibid.

MIES

JOHNSON

MIES

JOHNSON

CORB

INSTRUCTIONS

TROTTER—

Joseph Wright of Derby, *An Experiment
on a Bird in the Air Pump*, 1768.

a discrete understanding of architectural activity and recapture "the higher ideal of unity as a more intimate working out of the expression of one's life in one's environment";[31] he pointed out that while "forces may be blind forever," humans can have no such luxury of perpetual indifference.[32]

And earlier, while Victorians were appropriating their landscape and their architecture as aesthetic constructs, scientists were discovering that life both within and without greenhouses was dependent on pneumatic (and therefore pollutable) currents.[33] In the eighteenth century, Joseph Wright of Derby's painting, *An Experiment on a Bird in the Air Pump*, did not simply describe what Joseph Priestley had elucidated with his discovery of dephlogisticated air in 1771: that, as Otto von Guericke declared after inventing the vacuum pump a century before, "a clock in a vacuum cannot be heard to strike; a flame dies out in it; a bird opens its bill wide, struggles for air, and dies."[34] Rather, the painting was also a map of the increasingly efficient interdependence between ecology, art, science, technology and economic-industrial

capitalization. Wright's ability to support himself financially was dependent on the technological-fiscal success of members of the Lunar Society, which was, in turn, supported by the scientific achievements of men like Priestley, who functioned as a paid consultant to the group. Going back further, the science of the seventeenth century also cast doubt on the idea that life could spontaneously generate in sealed vessels; Francesco Redi's famous experiment with rotting meat and maggots illustrated that some exposure to the exterior insect life of air was necessary for the generation of larvae.[35] While architectural thinkers were busy building themselves larger and more impermeable containers, science was discovering that perfect enclosure also meant fatal suffocation, and that life did not spring from the inherent properties of inert substances but was always an infection of foreign material.

Even within Alberti's fifteenth-century conceptualization of mind and nature, tension existed. While the *procedure* of architectural production was now divided into mind and matter, the *result* of this practice was the origin at which the earthy abscissa and the abstract ordinate intersected and could be re-cognized as a harmonious whole. In *De Re Aedificatoria*, the ultimate evidence that

31– Ibid., 19.

32– Frank Lloyd Wright, "Architecture as a Profession Is All Wrong" [1930], *Frank Lloyd Wright: Collected Writings*, ed. Bruce Brooks Pfeiffer (New York: Rizzoli, 1992), 334.

33– Henry Smith Williams, *The Story of Nineteenth-Century Science* (New York: Harper and Brothers, 1900), 39.

34– Joseph Mayer, *The Seven Seals of Science: An Account of the Unfoldment of Orderly Knowledge and Its Influence on Human Affairs* (New York: Century Co., 1927), 109.

35– Ibid.

a favorable site had been discovered was the synthetic well-being of all the human, nonhuman, organic and inorganic elements, including everything from the paving stones and the trees to the health of babies and the spleen of cattle, and even the general wear of other buildings in the vicinity.[36] The separation between mind and matter was therefore incomplete from the beginning, achieved in the newly ordered process of architecture and in the newly minted definition of the architect himself, but relinquished when architecture and the landscape were ultimately reconstituted into a larger bionetwork of health and disease. Thus, paradoxically, the product of architectural commodification in the Renaissance returned its inhabitants to the interconnected pullulation of utterly uncategorizable ecology in the end.

Perhaps it is also useful for us to recall that there was another "renaissance" before Alberti's celebrated age of humanism. In the twelfth century, monastic medieval scholars abandoned their isolated reliance on crumbling and distant Christian texts and sought out Greek and Arabic mathematics, natural science and philosophy. These premodern intellectuals looked *outside* their own socioeconomic systems, cultural heritage and politico-religious traditions for knowledge and beauty as much as the fifteenth-century thinkers and their successors facilitated the interior relocation of this same material. The architectural co-development of the Middle Ages was also exterior: the great Gothic cathedrals, urban centers and agricultural *Landschaften* were outgrowths of a larger synthetic attitude towards shaping the environment and of a society in which skills were separate but

activities were common.[37] This preprofessional approach, so removed from our own education, may be the best model we have for the shifts we will have to make in a post-interior landscape.

So, to use Alberti's famous motto, *quid tum*? In an exterior of mutual contingencies, building on whatever material scale (we know that imagination and digital projection are also material) is a kind of cultivation. The fully relational landscape which we know ourselves to inhabit today makes it obvious that too much knowledge and too many different kinds and scales of expertise are required to continue to silo human involvement in the universe into discrete categories. Any recurrent desire to view architecture as protected, within art or itself or any other interior, has been revealed as simply facilitating its detachment from its only and inevitable lifelines. When, as Peter Sloterdijk has described, even the air we breathe and the water we drink are not easy givens, we cannot return to Alberti's quaint prescriptions that architecture ought to be built only where the water is clear and the air is pure. In our new perception, architecture is

36— Alberti I.3–6 (Rykwert 9–18).
37— See W. Sauerländer, "Renaissance of the Twelfth Century? Changing Perspectives in the Evaluation of Architectural History," *Sewanee Medieval Colloquium Occasional Papers*, II (1985): 25–29.

once again part of everything because we are forced to see everything as part of us.[38] At the same time, the pseudo-parrhesiaste classification of design as variously performalist, projective, sustainable, organicist, et cetera, has merely crudely mapped architectural creativity for its own taxation by real and indifferent forces. The corpus of architectural practice and discourse, so long seen as delineating, inhabiting, creating and extending interiority, has itself become trapped in a vacuum of its own imagination, depleting rapidly of oxygen while outside forces restlessly put out feelers in other directions.

In the context of the Holocene perspective to which we have been irretrievably exposed by recent discoveries, the construction, evolution and proleptic collapse of a professional architectural interior has been brief. This moment urgently presents a choice of whether the discourse and practice of architecture should blindly pretend to continue to construe architecture as an interior—a glass house in a static landscape—or should recognize and act upon the fact that it too can be a virus in the pulsing exterior life of everything else. Once released from its illusory conservatory, architecture, like all creative activity, is capable of fashioning and releasing negentropic forces in the surrounding catastrophes of socioeconomic, political and ecological instability. Break the glass.

38— Peter Sloterdijk, "Excerpts from Spheres III: Foams," trans. Daniela Fabricius, *Harvard Design Magazine* 29 (Fall/Winter 2008–9): 38–52.

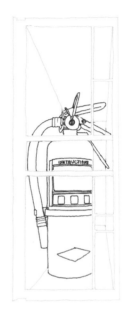

Contributors—

Esther Choi, an artist and writer, is Assistant Professor in the Departments of Criticism and Curatorial Practices and Photography at the Ontario College of Art and Design.

Marrikka Trotter is Founder of the Department of Micro-Urbanism and a PhD student in the history and theory of architecture at Harvard University.

Brett Albert is a recent graduate of the Harvard Graduate School of Design. He is currently living in suburban Ohio, plotting his revenge.

Matthew Allen is a disciplinarian and recent graduate of the Harvard Graduate School of Design.

Teddy Cruz is the principal of Estudio Teddy Cruz and an Associate Professor at the University of California, San Diego.

Suzanne Ernst is a landscape architect at PLANT Architect Inc.

Liam Gillick is an artist and writer based in New York and London.

K. Michael Hays is Eliot Noyes Professor of Architectural Theory at the Harvard Graduate School of Design.

Sanford Kwinter is Professor of Architectural Theory and Criticism and co-Director of the Master in Design Studies program at the Harvard Graduate School of Design.

Sylvia Lavin is the Chair of the PhD in Architecture Program and Professor of History and Theory at UCLA.

Michael Meredith is a principal at MOS and an Associate Professor at the Harvard Graduate School of Design.

Yu Morishita is a PhD student at the University of Tokyo Graduate School of Interdisciplinary Information Studies.

Trevor Patt is an instructor and researcher at the École Polytechnique Fédérale de Lausanne.

Philippe Rahm is the principal at Philippe Rahm Architects and Professor at École Cantonale d'Art de Lausanne.

Joe Ringenberg is a recent graduate of the Harvard Graduate School of Design. "I am quite content to go down to posterity as a scissors and paste man." (James Joyce)

Jonathan Tate is a partner at buildingstudio, principal of Miscellaneous Tactics and an Adjunct Assistant Professor at Tulane University.

Douglas Wu is a real estate investment banker at HSBC in Hong Kong. He recently earned his MArch degree from the Harvard Graduate School of Design.

Cover Photograph: Esther Choi, 2009. © Esther Choi. Image courtesy of the artist.

ii–iii   Joe Ringenberg, *Plan*, 2010. © Joe Ringenberg. Image courtesy of the artist.

2–3   Esther Choi, *Vertigo* [Detail], 2009. © Esther Choi. Image courtesy of the author.

4–5   Esther Choi, *Pressure Waves*, 2009. © Esther Choi. Image courtesy of the author.

6–7   Esther Choi, *Oblique*, 2009. © Esther Choi. Image courtesy of the author.

8–9   Esther Choi, *Vertigo*, 2009. © Esther Choi. Image courtesy of the author.

11   Architecture Principe, Église Sainte-Bernadette du Banlay, Nevers, France, 1966. © Bruno Bellec. Image courtesy of the photographer.

Esther Choi, *Sketch of Church Sainte-Bernadette du Banlay*, 2009. © Esther Choi. Image courtesy of the author.

12   Hans Haacke, *The Invisible Hand of the Market*, 2009. Installation, text, moving image of hand, empty lockers. Dimensions variable. Text panel with hand: 55.2 x 543.6 x 25.4 cm. Installation image from Hans Haacke: *Weather, or Not*, X Initiative, New York, NY (November 21, 2009–February 6, 2010). ©2010 Hans Haacke/Artists Rights Society (ARS), New York/VG Bild-Kunst, Bonn. Image courtesy of Paula Cooper Gallery. Photograph by Tom Powel Imaging Inc., New York.

Hans Haacke, *Recording of Climate in Art Exhibition*, 1969–1970/2009. Hygrothermograph, barograph, and chart paper. Chart paper: measuring at 7 day increments and pinned to the wall each week of exhibition. Hygrothermograph: 29.8 x 33.3 x 17.1 cm. Barograph: 29.2 x 31.1 x 14 cm. © 2010 Hans Haacke/Artists Rights Society (ARS), New York/VG Bild-Kunst, Bonn. Image courtesy of Paula Cooper Gallery.

Hans Haacke, *BONUS-Storm*, 2009. Installation: flashing light box and six wall-mounted industrial fans. Light box: 121.9 x 182.9 x 16.5 cm. Fans (each): 83.8 cm diameter x 45.7 cm depth. © 2010 Hans Haacke/Artists Rights Society (ARS), New York/VG Bild-Kunst, Bonn. Image courtesy of Paula Cooper Gallery.

12–13   Esther Choi, *Oblique* [Detail], 2009. © Esther Choi. Image courtesy of the author.

14–15   Esther Choi, *Houndstooth Haze and Pressure Waves*, 2009. © Esther Choi. Image courtesy of the author.

22–23   SANAA, Rolex Learning Center, EPFL, Lausanne, Switzerland, 2009. © Trevor Patt. Image courtesy of the photographer.

26–27   Matthew Allen, *Sketch of Seijo* [Exterior view], 2009. © Matthew Allen. Image courtesy of the author.

28–29   Matthew Allen, *Sketch of Seijo* [Interior view], 2009. © Matthew Allen. Image courtesy of the author.

30–31   Matthew Allen, *Sketch of Seijo* [Interior view], 2009. © Matthew Allen. Image courtesy of the author.

32   Kazuyo Sejima & Associates, SeijoTownhouses, Tokyo, Japan, 2007. © Iwan Baan. Image courtesy of the photographer.

44–45   Paul Andreu, The National Grand Theater, Beijing, China, 2007. © Manuela Martin. Image courtesy of the photographer.

46–47   Herzog and de Meuron, Beijing National Stadium, Beijing, China, 2008. © David Brittain. Image courtesy of the photographer.

48–49   Douglas Wu, *Horse Character Evolution*, 2009. © Douglas Wu. Images courtesy of the author.

50–51   Douglas Wu, *Fish Character Evolution*, 2009. © Douglas Wu. Images courtesy of the author.

52–53 Douglas Wu, *Car Character Evolution*, 2009. © Douglas Wu. Images courtesy of the author.

54–55 C. Y. Lee, Pangu Plaza, Beijing, China, 2008. © Aimin Wang. Image courtesy of the photographer.

56–57 Foster + Partners, Beijing Capital International Airport, Beijing, China, 2008. © Nigel Young / Foster + Partners. Image courtesy of Foster + Partners.

59 Gensler, Shanghai Tower, Shanghai, China, c. 2014. © Gensler. Image courtesy of Gensler.

62–63 Brett Albert, *Housing Skins* [Detail], 2009. © Brett Albert. Image courtesy of the author.

64–65 Brett Albert, *Housing Skins* [Detail], 2009. © Brett Albert. Image courtesy of the author.

65 Assadi and Pulido, Guthrie House, Santiago, Chile, 2007. © Guy Wenborne. Image courtesy of the photographer.

66 Brett Albert, *Housing Skins* [Detail], 2009. © Brett Albert. Image courtesy of the author.

68–69 Brett Albert, *Housing Skins* [Detail], 2009. © Brett Albert. Image courtesy of the author.

69 *NIKEiD*, 2010. http://nikeid.nike.com/nikeid. © Nike. Image courtesy of Nike Media Relations.

70–71 Brett Albert, *Housing Skins*, 2009. © Brett Albert. Image courtesy of the author.

72–73 Brett Albert, *Housing Skins* [Detail], 2009. © Brett Albert. Image courtesy of the author.

84–85 László Egyed, *Untitled*, 2010. © László Egyed. Image courtesy of the photographer.

86 Suzanne Ernst, *Gold Passage 2*, 2008. © Suzanne Ernst. Image courtesy of the author.

88–89 Suzanne Ernst, *Gold Passage*, 2008. © Suzanne Ernst. Image courtesy of the author.

90–91 Suzanne Ernst, *Gold Brocade*, 2008. © Suzanne Ernst. Image courtesy of the author.

91 Suzanne Ernst, *Patio*, 2008. © Suzanne Ernst. Image courtesy of the author.

92–93 Suzanne Ernst, *Brocade and Safety*, 2009. © Suzanne Ernst. Image courtesy of the author.

93 Suzanne Ernst, *Security and Gold Lines*, 2009. © Suzanne Ernst. Image courtesy of the author.

94–95 Suzanne Ernst, *Security and Passage*, 2009. © Suzanne Ernst. Image courtesy of the author.

108–109 Yu Morishita, *Eitoku Study* [Detail], 2009. © Yu Morishita. Image courtesy of the author.

112–113 Yu Morishita, *Kyoto Wells and Canals*, 2009. © Yu Morishita. Image courtesy of the author.

116 Eitoku Kanō, *Uesugi-Bon Rakuchu-Rakugai-Zu Byōbu*, 1565. Pair of six panel folding screens; ink, pigment, and gold on gilded paper, 160.5 x 323.5 cm. Image courtesy of Yonezawa City Uesugi Museum.

116–117 Yu Morishita, *Eitoku Study*, 2009. © Yu Morishita. Image courtesy of the author.

118–119 Evita Yumul, *Kyoto dots*, 2009. © Evita Yumul. Image courtesy of the artist.

122 Joe Ringenberg, *Razzle Savoye*, 2008. © Joe Ringenberg. Image courtesy of the author.

123 Joe Ringenberg, *Graph Paper Wall*, 2008. © Joe Ringenberg. Image courtesy of the author.

124 Julia Rothman, *Liontile*, 2008. © Julia Rothman. Image courtesy of the artist. www.juliarothman.com

125 Julia Rothman, *Liontile, Grey and Blue*, 2008. © Julia Rothman. Image courtesy of the artist. www.juliarothman.com

126 Wim Delvoye, *Louise*, 2004. Taxidermied tattooed pig, 115 x 37 x 59 cm. © Wim Delvoye. Image courtesy of Wim Delvoye Studio.

127 Joe Ringenberg, *MASS Map Collage*, 2008. © Joe Ringenberg. Image courtesy of the author.

128–129 Joe Ringenberg, *Nolli and CCTV Collage*, 2008. © Joe Ringenberg. Image courtesy of the author.

138 Trevor Patt, Line diagram of Tony Garnier's *Une Cité Industrielle*, 2009. © Trevor Patt. Image courtesy of the author.

139 Trevor Patt, Line diagrams of Tony Garnier, *Une Cité Industrielle* (1917); Ebenezer Howard, *Garden City* (1898); Le Corbusier, *Ville Contemporaine* (1922); Frank Lloyd Wright, *Broadacre City* (1932–1959); Peter Cook, *Plug-in City* (1964), 2009. © Trevor Patt. Images courtesy of the author.

141 Albert Robida, *Un quartier embrouillé* from *Le vingtième siècle: la vie électrique*, c.1883. Colored engraving. Image courtesy of Harvard College Library Digital Imaging Group, 2010: 90W–205 F, Houghton Library, Harvard University.

142 Eugène Hénard, *Rue Future*, 1910, from "The Cities of the Future," *American City*, Volume 4, January, 1911. Image from the collection of Loeb Design Library, Harvard University.

144–147 Trevor Patt, *Skycar City* [Sketch]. 2006. Courtesy of UWM's Marcus Prize Studio, 2006, co-led by Winy Maas and Grace La.

150–151 Eugène Hénard, *Rue Future* [Detail], 1910, from "The Cities of the Future," *American City*, Volume 4, January, 1911. Image from the collection of Loeb Design Library, Harvard University.

160–161 Philip Johnson, Glass House, New Canaan, Connecticut, 1949. © Melody Kramer. Image courtesy of the photographer.

162 Marrikka Trotter, *Medieval woodcut with the Glass House*, 2010. © Marrikka Trotter. Image courtesy of the author.

163 Andrea Palladio, View of the main facade of San Francesco della Vigna, Venice, Italy,

c. 1564. Photo Credit: Cameraphoto Arte, Venice / Art Resource, NY.

164 Marrikka Trotter, *The Glass House as Nuremberg Surrounded by its Managed Forests*, 2010. © Marrikka Trotter. Image courtesy of the author.

165 Robert Hooke, *Hooke's observations of the cellular structure of cork and a sprig of Sensible (Sensitive) Plant*, 1665. Location: Oxford Science Archive, Oxford, Great Britain. Photo Credit: Oxford Science Archive / HIP / Art Resource, NY.

167 Marrikka Trotter, *Tintern Abbey and the Glass House through a Claude Glass*, 2010. © Marrikka Trotter. Image courtesy of the author.

168 Marrikka Trotter, *The Glass House in a Greenhouse*, 2010. © Marrikka Trotter. Image courtesy of the author.

169 Marrikka Trotter, *Mies, Johnson, Corb: The Glass House as a MOMA Model*, 2010. © Marrikka Trotter. Image courtesy of the author.

172–173 Marrikka Trotter, *Glass House Sketches*, 2010. © Marrikka Trotter. Image courtesy of the author.

174 Joseph Wright of Derby, *An Experiment on a Bird in the Air Pump*, 1768. Oil on canvas, 183 x 244 cm. Location: National Gallery, London. Photo Credit: © National Gallery, London / Art Resource, NY.

175 Marrikka Trotter, *An Experiment on a Bird in the Glass House*, 2010. © Marrikka Trotter. Image courtesy of the author.

177 Marrikka Trotter, *In Case of Emergency Break the Glass House*, 2010. © Marrikka Trotter. Image courtesy of the author.

200–201 Joe Ringenberg, *Elevation*, 2010. © Joe Ringenberg. Image courtesy of the artist.

Index

Page numbers in italics refer to illustrations.

A note on type

The book is primarily set in Akzidenz-Grotesk Medium, a typeface originally released by the Berthold foundry in 1896. It quickly became one of the most widely used sans-serifs and later inspired and served as the basis for a number of modern typefaces including Helvetica and Univers. The secondary type used in the conversations is Monospace 821, designed by Max Miedinger in 1957. The fixed-width or monospace font was originally designed for typewriters and is used in the conversations to reference the forms of transcription and informal correspondence.